At The Pinnacle

One Woman's Running Journey

Erika Abraham

Copyright © 2018 by Erika Abraham

All rights reserved.

No part of this book may be reproduced in any form or by any electronic or mechanical means including information storage and retrieval systems, without permission in writing from the author. The only exception is by a reviewer, who may quote short excerpts in a review.

Editor, Cover Design: Greg Schaffer
Cover Painting: Heidi Rieper

ISBN-978-0-9911052-8-1
10 9 8 7 6 5 4 3 2 1

This book is dedicated to the four special guys in my life, husband Roy and sons David, Paul, and Greg. They inspired me to reach all of life's finish lines standing up and smiling.

A special note of thanks to my twin sister, Heidi Rieper. Her oil painting of the cover design captures the spirit of my running journey.

Contents

Foreword i
Preface v
Chapter One - At the Starting Line 1
Chapter Two - The Lighter Side of Running 15
Chapter Three - If the Shoe Fits 41
Chapter Four - Footsteps in Double Time 51
Chapter Five - Missteps (Or Missed Steps) 63
Chapter Six - Variations on the Theme 91
Chapter Seven - Soaring with the Turkeys 109
Chapter Eight - Shifting Gears and Footstrikes . 131
Chapter Nine - Beyond The Ordinary 143
Chapter Ten - Bring Back Pheidippides 171
Chapter Eleven - Catch the Racing Spirit 217
Chapter Twelve - High Anxiety 233
Chapter Thirteen - Reflections 261
Epilogue 289
Addendum - Records 291

Foreword

I was riding in the back seat of the 1971 Chevy Vega, enjoying my usual daily ferry from my grandmother's house where my aunt looked after me while my mother worked to support three young boys. My older brothers were old enough to be left on their own, at least in terms of early 1970s suburban New York culture. I, on the other hand, at the tender age of six, required constant supervision.

On that trip home, I remember riding in the backseat looking at my mom from behind, noticing a tear on her cheek, as we drove from the Sunoco gas station towards the Bronx River Parkway. I thought that maybe the long wait in the gas line had upset her, but we had no choice, as the Vega's license plate dictated gas today or a couple of days later. The wait hadn't done much for me, either. I had places to go and television to see – Star Trek was on at 6 PM on channel 11, and if we didn't hurry, I'd miss the first part of it.

As young children, we tend to keep fresh snippets of memories that profoundly affect us. I suppose that many of these powerful snapshots in time stay with us our entire life, as this one did with me. I don't know if I asked her a question or if she volunteered information. All I remember is her saying that one day my father will realize the mistake he made and come back, and she will not accept him. I did not know what to say. I probably said nothing. Her words didn't make me sad, but her sadness permeated me. I can still feel that moment deep inside, now 44 or so years later.

Roughly twenty-seven years after that emotional twenty minute car ride back to our small apartment, we stood together at the start of the first Country Music Marathon in Nashville, Tennessee. For me, running the 26.2 miles was a bucket-list item. For her, it represented another 26.2 miles in what had become a long journey for her, one footstrike at a time. I remember her being happy at the start, me not so much, as I was not sure if I could prevail. Yet whenever I faced uncertainty, Mom had a knack of offering genuine encouragement. This was no exception. Why should it be?

She was right, of course. I did not spontaneously implode, though my right big toe took a beating. Her words of encouragement had stayed with me mile after mile. I limped across the finish line a couple of minutes ahead of her, how I have no idea, but I had finished. Her husband Roy, whom she met at the early stages of her running saga 12 years earlier, took the photos of the victorious, and Mom submitted one to Runner's World Magazine as part of a short interest article. When I asked her why she had chosen an image where I looked like I was in distress, she said that they were all like that. Of course, she was beaming in all of the pictures.

This was not the sad person I remembered from the drive home in the early 1970s. She had become a happy, confident, vibrant, alive person. What had changed? She had discovered running.

I had the pleasure of a front-seat view of the transformation my mother, Erika Abraham, from sad, recently divorced mother of three to one who possessed much confidence and vigor. She had sacrificed pretty much everything for her three sons. When the last one (me) had proven himself able to exist outside the comfort of the nest, she finally began to focus more on herself. Boy, did she ever!

This book chronicles the evolution of many aspects of her running journey in a manner that is uplifting, humorous, and most of all, inspiring. Adapting running articles she had penned over several decades, At The Pinnacle is a unique biography of one woman, beaten but never defeated, who found a spark that ignited a flame that grew into a roaring bonfire that is still burning strong. She made it to the top and stayed there!

Before I close, I need to address a few things:
- My sixteen-year-old, mulleted, insecure self was in fact worried what peers may think if they saw me running with her. Silly me.
- I will never, ever come close to her PRs, in any distance.
- I can't say I'm too old to run anymore as she's still running regularly as she approaches 80. Thanks, Mom!

She is the best runner in the family, the pillar of strength and endurance that we all draw from, both on the road and off. What a pleasure, privilege, and blessing to have this absolutely remarkable person as my mother. Enjoy and draw inspiration from her unique story, and always finish upright and smiling!

Greg Schaffer
March 2018

Preface

"I've learned that you can keep going long after you think you can't." - Author Unknown

About Me - Becoming a Runner

After a heartbreaking divorce in 1971, I was a sad single Mom, broken in spirit, whose life revolved around raising three young sons, tiring work hours, and endless college studies. Smiles and fun times were elusive. In 1981, after ten arduous years, I earned my AAS Degree in Medical Lab Technology and my BS in Biology. Steps in the right direction.

In the early 1980s, I dabbled in leisurely running on residential streets wearing white Converse sneakers for footwear. Nothing serious, just ensuing sore feet and aching limbs. This was later followed by a few runs "off the beaten path" i.e. in hidden fields (1983 - 1985) in Binghamton with my faster, more energetic, and impatient youngest teenaged son (Greg). Since I owned no special athletic attire, he made it known that he did not want to be seen running with a Mom whose outfits were not stylish or color matched. These runs were mercifully short-lived due to my depleted stamina after working two jobs. Sadness, loneliness, and financial challenges prevailed. However, on Easter Sunday in 1985, a bright spot loomed on the horizon. With wishful thinking, I said to my middle son (Paul) who was home on a college break, "Someday I hope to run the New York City Marathon." Without hesitation he replied, "Go for it, Mom!" Thus a dream was born.

In late 1985 I accepted a new lab job offer from my former employer and returned to Rockland County, later earning the title of Research and Development Scientist/Chemist. On April Fool's Day in 1986, at age nearly 48, I accepted the challenge of a much younger co-worker to go for a short run at a nearby local park. From this start I earned an unusual moniker, and the legend of "Wonder Weed" was born.

On November 1, 1987, wearing a pale pink T-shirt with ERIKA printed on the front and WONDER WEED on the back, along with shocking pink terry cloth shorts, I completed my first New York City Marathon in a time of 4:48:59. From then on running took center stage in my life. On a cold January day in 1988 I met an equally avid runner named Roy. Together we ran the 1988/1989 New Year's Eve Midnight Run in Central Park, complete with fireworks at midnight and cups of free champagne on the course. True to form, Roy proposed as we crossed the finish line of this five mile race.

I was born to run, having a Mom who could out-walk anyone and a Dad whose dream of running for Germany in the 1936 Berlin Olympics was derailed by Hitler. In February 1994 I was honored by the New York Road Runners Club as their 1993 Masters B (55-59) Runner of the year.

Still, I was a singular runner with a drive to do my best. Running has always been in my blood, I knew, and I loved sharing my passion with others. However, I did not realize, though, the positive influence I had become to others. In 2013, I was surprised to learn that the Mid-Hudson Road Runners Club saw me as a role model and at the Treetops to Rooftops 5K presented the first annual SPIRIT OF ERIKA ABRAHAM AWARD, given annually to a youthful runner who has demonstrated a similar passion and commitment to running. The recipient mirrors my tenacious dedication to the sport, including many marathons and ultras, overcoming obstacles with a smile at the finish, despite the struggles met along the way. I am honored and humbled to serve as an inspiration to the next generations of runners. Additionally in 2013, the local Lions Club honored me with a Lifetime Achievement Award For The Sport of Running.

I hope this brief summary of my running journey, eventually having completed distances of 100 meters on the track to marathons and ultramarathons, can inspire everyone. For me, it has been an incredible journey of courage, tenacity, determination, self-discoveries, an enduring spirit, camaraderie, special friendships, unlimited smiles, and success beyond my wildest dreams. As these words of Michael Korda so eloquently state, "In order to succeed we must first believe that we can." How true these words proved to be for me.

Chapter One - At the Starting Line

"Life before 50 is nothing but a warm-up." – Modern Maturity Magazine, December 1993 – January 1994 issue

How I Started Running

I guess I like to move in the fast lane. Way back when, as an eighth grader, I was a first string guard on our school's basketball team. Although not described as poetry in motion I was fast on my feet and covered a lot of ground on the court. Later that year my twin sister and I anchored the last two legs of our school's winning relay team. We were real speedsters that day, she being the fastest.

Fast forward to 1985 in Binghamton. I tried some brief running with my youngest son, then age 17 and a fashion-conscious lad. We ran when and where his high school peers wouldn't see him with me. You see, my running attire failed big time in the "making a fashion statement" category. My clothes were not of the designer label variety nor were they color-coordinated. Sometime thereafter I wistfully expressed my desire to someday run the New York City Marathon to my middle son, Paul. His quick enthusiastic response was "Go for it, Mom." Yeah, right.

Fast forward again to Rockland County on April 1, 1986, a few weeks before my 48th birthday. A much younger co-worker challenged me to run with her at

Rockland Lake State Park doing about a mile of the three mile inner loop. Picture me in my work attire consisting of dark brown polyester slacks, a tan top with the Florida Keys logo emblazoned in bright orange, and Lord only knows what kind of footwear. I was afraid to show my legs. I must have been quite a sight being barely able to breathe and struggling to put one foot in front of the other at her pace. Thank God she opted to walk back. That one mile run left me gasping for air, quite sore, and with a determination to run better the "next time around."

Running at the lake became an almost daily challenge for me. By early May 1986 I could easily run two complete loops (six miles) with more speed. My only pair of shorts was of the shocking pink terry cloth variety. Certainly no fashion statement!

On August 3, 1986, four months after hitting the pavement, I was ready to run my first race, a 5K. Can you picture this naive runner taking great pains to center her bib number on the back of her T-shirt? With jitters, a nervous stomach, and aching legs I finished the course in 26:08, placing 5th in the 40-49 age group. Shortly thereafter I ran my first 10K race in 50:29, placed 3rd in my age group and was awarded a beautiful bronze medal. It was the shock of my life that I could actually win something for running. Little did I know then of the magnitude of awards that racing would bring me in the years that followed.

Running was therapeutic. It replaced the heartbreak of a 1971 divorce and a life of "kids, work, and school" with inner peace, renewed energy, a new level of confidence, and grins that could match those of the

Cheshire Cat. This wilted flower finally started to bloom. Imagine getting wolf-whistles at the age of 49! So, I kept on running and running and running.

By November 1987 I was ready for my first 26.2 miler, the New York City Marathon. My pink shorts and T-shirt were earlier described as not giving a boost to the fashion industry. My two oldest sons (David and Paul) met me at various places along the course and cheered me on. When I approached Columbus Circle my middle son left the viewing stands and leaped over the barrier to join me but a policeman quickly steered him away from my side. I can still recall his pleading words to no avail, "But she's my Mom." I finished in 4:48:59.

Since that April Fool's Day in 1986 I have put many miles on my feet, won countless awards, and learned, albeit slowly, to like the person that I was. The brown polyester slacks and pink terry cloth shorts have long since been discarded. Through running I blossomed into the person I am today. Through running, talents that had been relegated to the back burner emerged. Recognition in art and journalism followed.

I can now look back with humor at those early years of running. A klutz on the roads for sure! All of my moveable parts ached at one time or another. It was truly the agony of de feet, de bones, de legs, de arms, etc. Running was more than a way of life. It was the chance to be myself, to test my strengths, and to pursue my goals. It was the freedom to be the "me" who I wanted to be. Running literally gave me back my life and, years later, gave me my husband, Roy.

Dr. George Sheehan once said, "Out on the roads there is fitness and self-discovery and the persons we were destined to be." It's true that we are only beaten when we stop believing who we wish we can be.

On The "Short" Side

One of the beautiful benefits of running is the camaraderie and friendships formed with other runners. This is a story about a friendship formed through the common bond of running and initiated by an unusual pair of shorts.

To the trained and "real" runner, they looked out of place. To me, the novice runner, they were the only item available to wear. Their color was shocking, their texture passé. Their era of being "in" already went by the wayside.

I'm referring to my first (and one and only!) pair of running shorts. When one's first attempt at running is done on a whim and in response to a challenge from a co-worker and while wearing brown slacks, you know the runner is a novice or a nut. Well, that was me back on April Fool's Day in 1986 when I first started pounding the pavement. This, therefore, puts the wearing of the shorts in proper perspective.

When the slacks became too uncomfortable and hot for running, I switched to those shocking pink terry cloth shorts. I shudder at the running fashion statement that I must have made! However, they served a useful purpose for someone on a limited budget . . . and they were the reason behind my meeting a special friend.

Looking back, I recall how many running memories these out of place and out of style pink terry cloth shorts shared with me. They saw me through my first competitive running races. For my second race and first ever 10K they were with me when I won a third place 40-49 age group award. This is where my story actually begins.

It was at this 10K race that I met one of my special friends, who introduced herself and asked to see my medal. You guessed it! Behind it all was that pair of pink terry cloth shorts. As she later admitted, she didn't think anyone wearing those shorts could be a serious runner!

We met for the second time at my next 10K race in Ringwood, New Jersey. You're right - it was the pink terry cloth shorts again that helped her recognize me. I won the first place 40-49 age group award and she placed second. We laughed about my shorts while elatedly comparing trophy sizes.

Soon we were comparing running notes. Going further, we discovered that our lives had crossed similar paths. We were both single parents and we were both employed in the scientific field, she as a high school chemistry teacher and I as a Research and Development Scientist/Chemist. She had one son, I had three.

The more we talked, the more we learned that we had much in common. Our running "careers" started at about the same time. We also shared this newly-found passion for running and racing. This was the glue that cemented our friendship - despite the outdated pink terry cloth shorts.

I later wore the shorts at my first New York City Marathon in 1987. To make them more comfortable for running, I cut a side slit on each leg opening. This facilitated leg movement but did not make a lasting impression on the sports fashion industry. A finish line photo forever preserves their memory.

The shorts in question are long gone. They have been replaced by black lycra tri-shorts, purple Moving Comfort ones, and other assorted types and colors.

I am thankful for running and for the pink shorts for bringing me this friendship. Although I have since met many more wonderful people through running, none were brought about as uniquely as this one.

The Agony and Ecstasy of a First-Time Marathon Runner

Brain, think! Why did you ever convince me that I could run a marathon? Hasn't my body been used and abused enough? Now you tell me to "go for it" when, in a moment of insanity, I toyed with a fleeting idea about maybe trying my first 26.2 miler. Now you want me to endure the ultimate punishment and actually do it? Insanity has taken over and I give in to this crazy notion.

Training runs start, and so does the agony of pounding the pavement with a leg injury. Is there ecstasy in all this nonsense? Training runs continue. My legs perform unwillingly as the weekly miles increase. Bit by slow, painful bit, my legs and body begin a quasi-acceptance of the abuse I chose to put them through. In the pre-sunrise stages of the early morning and post-sunset stages of the early evening I run. I go steady with the roosters and the owls. As I wage my battle to run so does the rest of my body. It wages a different battle. It's agony.

The day of the big event arrives. Hey, what am I doing here in this mass of humanity on Staten Island? My spirit is willing but my flesh is sooooo weak! I may have many little battles along the way but this is sheer madness. Combating butterflies in my stomach and wobbly knees, I impatiently wait in line at a portable toilet as hunger pains overtake me. A squished banana and crackers to the rescue!

As I survey my surroundings a United Nations of runners engulfs me. Everywhere there are runners of all shapes, sizes, and colors. A potpourri of America. I glance upward and see bare-leafed trees decorated with a multitude of gaily colored garments carelessly (or not so carelessly) flung there. Christmas in November, I wonder? Liniment tubes, lonely socks, a misplaced glove or two, caps, bandanas of the well-worn variety, and whatnot all cover the heavily trodden sod. Like a mass exodus, the assembly to the starting area begins. I'm scared.

Hey, I'm on the beautiful Verrazano-Narrows Bridge, my legs are cruising through the streets of Brooklyn and across the Pulaski Bridge. On and on I run. WOW! This is fun! So many spectators call my name that I feel famous.

Uh oh, I don't like this. It goes up and up and up. Now tell me where the top of the 59th Street Bridge is. It is said that ignorance is bliss. Well, I'm very ignorant but this certainly isn't bliss. Ouch, the grid under the carpeting is penetrating the soles of my running shoes and my aching calves are waging their own private battle with pain.

I'm so hungry that I'm grabbing all the free food handouts I can get. Oh shucks, a nauseous stomach entered the arena. Whew! Saved by a gas station on First Avenue. I'm now so hungry I can eat the paper cups off the street! Amidst the agony I can only think of FOOD and FINISH.

Yippee, I made it! Central Park at last! Uh, oh, what's this up ahead? NOT ANOTHER HILL! I'm tired of hilly surprises. Why am I leaving the park? How will I find the finish line?

Whew! I'm back in the park again. The crowds seem to cheer louder. I see the huge colorful marathon banner and clock looming ahead. I'm at the finish line and it's over. I did it! Now where's the food?

Afterwards, I chuckled as I thought about these words: "The human body has several hundred muscles, mostly to tell us we shouldn't have jogged so far." – The Idea Treasury

Remembering My First (and Only) Triathlon

It's spring 1988 and I am running my third and last lap around the three mile inner loop at Rockland Lake. A running friend who has just been accepted into the prestigious Ironman Triathlon expounds the benefits and joys of being a triathlete. I am bitten by the bug. The run ends all too soon as does our conversation, but the thought of attempting a triathlon lingers on for me. When I ask Roy for his opinion he responds with an enthusiastic "I know you can do it." Now I can only silently wonder, "What am I getting myself into?"

Having not done any swimming in more years than I can remember I reluctantly "take to the water." Swimming doesn't come easy. My arms get tired and my legs resist the kicking movement. I swallow more water than I care to think about. As I survey the length of the pool that "oh, just let me sink" feeling sets in. I am definitely not a water person.

It isn't long, however, before I am actually swimming half lengths in the pool, secure in the safety of always reaching the sides. Since I am not sinking like a ball and chain I conclude that my unorthodox swimming style must be working. I am encouraged to continue.

Soon I start cycling on my ancient three-speed bike. This joy is short-lived when I attempt to learn the rudiments of riding my brand new 12-speed Cannondale bicycle. It's true madness again. I am intimidated by this bike. I am frightened by the hand brakes (foot brakes are my strength), the dropped handlebars (how can I see where I am going?), the odd-looking toe clips, and that miserably placed cross bar on the frame. I look at the tiny seat and stare in wonderment. Me? Sit on that?

Roy's patience in teaching me the fundamentals of mastering this monster is unlimited. He knows that I have a mere six weeks to learn the gears and hone my biking skills before attempting my first triathlon. Another running friend sees me riding the bike instead of running and asks, "Are you injured?" "No," I respond. "I'm trying to learn how to ride this darn thing." Her chuckle is so refreshing . . . I think.

I somehow manage to train in all three disciplines. With two jobs, time management is a necessity. Swimming takes the starch out of me. A friend eases my fear of doing the swimming segment by saying, "Oh, that's the easy part. You can always fake it and doggy-paddle." I do some swimming at Lake Sebago where I learn about battling seaweed and being in ice cold water. My level of courage takes a roller-coaster ride. I do not like it one bit.

I miss the time to solely devote to running but my spirits are buoyed by beginning to like biking. I try longer distances, one-hand gear turning, and drinking from the water bottle. The monster bike becomes my friend as we keep company riding over hill and dale. Hey, this is fun after all!

Running keeps my sanity in check. It is my savior. It gives me the impetus to continue with all my training. Running clears my head. It tells me I can do it.

A perfect day dawns on August 21st and it is time to put my training to the test. I am grateful to be in the last wave for the half mile swim. I become some participants' battering ram during this segment. After two good head kicks and a foot caught in my bathing suit's strap, I fight back for my spot in the water. Soon I exit the water and head for the transition area. What a relief!

Wet clothes air dry on the bike segment. I remember steep uphills and wonderful cooling downhills. I may not be fast, but I plug away until I reach the transition area again after 16 miles of pedaling.

In rapid succession I am on the run yet feel that I am getting nowhere. My jelly legs do not want to move. Once I get up to speed I make up time and run a good five mile segment. Soon the finish line is in sight.

My combined time of 2:22:17 makes me an age group winner and qualifies me for an upcoming Big Apple Biathlon Championship in Central Park. I have the grin of the Cheshire Cat and am ecstatic. Roy gives me the "good job" nod and lets me rest on my laurels.

Chapter Two - The Lighter Side of Running

"A face without a smile is like a day without light." –
Author Unknown

The Caped Crusader of Sweat

My husband calls me "The Goddess of Running." I call him "Rancid Man." Just as Gotham City has Batman and Metropolis has Superman, the running community has its own caped crusader - Rancid Man!

We all sweat, and runners battling the summer heat and humidity get soaked and emit their own sweaty aroma. The perspiration douses their skin and clothes, drips relentlessly down their foreheads to their eyes, and, when really profuse, meanders down a wet path on their legs, finding its final resting place in their running shoes.

Your acute nasal passages may pick up a whiff of our caped hero's perspiration as he runs by. One quick visual glance tells you that he appears to have been drenched by a relentless downpour. Yet the sun has been shining brightly all day! His clothes are tightly pasted on him. His eyes squint in the sun to ward off the steady stream of salty perspiration that drips from his forehead like a rushing waterfall. When he pauses to rest a puddle forms instantly at his feet. His running shoes slosh like saturated sponges when he steps aside. He knows it may take many days for them to air out and thoroughly dry. Then they take on the appearance of a contorted sculpture - a remnant of some artist's worst nightmare.

In the wintertime, it's no better for this caped crusader of sweat. Despite the cold temperatures, his garments are soaked to the core. He becomes enshrouded in steam as he changes to drier clothing. He is an apparition from outer space as the steam follows his movements and footsteps. He is Rancid Man year 'round.

When I first saw this caped crusader of sweat approach me it was certainly not a vision of loveliness. As I stood there mute, he stretched out his long, soggy arms and boldly announced, "Here comes Rancid Man." "Yuk," I muttered in return, as the aroma of his sweat permeated the air. "Do I really want to be hugged by him?" Still, a hug is a hug, so his sweaty embrace wasn't turned down.

Now, whenever this caped crusader approaches the quizzical stares of other runners, he proudly announces his arrival with a resounding "It's a bird, it's a plane, it's Rancid Man!" In reality, it's another example of the off-beat humor of Roy.

Sometimes You Just Have To Laugh

This is about running, friendship, laughter... and strange sightings.

It happened during a weekly run with my good friend and fellow running club member. It was one of those days where we just needed to run. Blame it on work stress, life stress or just plain old stressed-out stress.

We needed to run, to chat, to console, to listen, and finally to laugh. After an overnight snowfall and morning rain, the temperature warmed up nicely and the roads were adequately dry, albeit icy in spots. We decided to do the "river run," a favorite scenic, low-key five mile course. The course crosses over small rivers, hence its name.

The rivers on the course each have a small bridge that we cross. These bridges are for pausing to stretch, admiring our surroundings, or talking about how high or how low the water is - just a nice pause that refreshes.

One river has in it what appears to be an airplane wing. Yes, a bona fide (we think!) airplane wing. We have not yet waded into the water to examine it and check out the rivets that mark its seams.

When the water is low, we can stop and view our airplane wing and exchange thoughts/words about when and how it might have gotten there. We can and do laugh at this strange sight. Other times the water is so high that we can't even see the hidden thing, yet we know it's there. So we pause again, share a laugh, stretch a bit, talk about the water, and then get on with our run. This marks the turnaround point on our running route.

Nearby there is a wooded trail used by mountain bikers, who we occasionally see. The main roadway has recently been repaved and widened with the addition of a slight hill. We've run past while the road work was in progress, waving a friendly "HI!" to the workers who often halted work machinery to allow us a safe passage. They became accustomed to seeing us on our weekly running treks. This day there were no workers.

On earlier runs, parts of the course were so wet and muddy that we didn't know where to plant our next footstrike. We became awkward ballerinas doing lopsided pirouettes. All the while, we could only laugh at how silly we must have looked.

Another time the new roadway was only partially completed, prompting us to seek out the "old" road. Much to our chagrin the "old" road came to a dead end at a high mound of dirt and rocks. Rather than turn back we climbed up this obstacle and laughed when we reached the top, only to find ourselves on the partially completed new road that we thought we could bypass.

This time, however, we needed to talk as we ran, to "clear off our chest." Friends can do that. So this day's run was just what we needed for tackling the stress.

Then we saw it!!! I don't know how we missed it earlier as we ran by. Perhaps we were on the other side of the road or too engrossed in our conversation as we ran. Yet there it was, this pretty wrapped package by the roadside. The wrapping was metallic royal blue tied with a blue and green ribbon. It was square in shape, solid and somewhat heavy. Of course, I picked it up, being ever so curious as to why a holiday-wrapped package would be left by the roadside. Hey, one never knows what treasures may confront a runner!

The final one and a half miles of our run involved wondering what the contents were. We guessed perhaps a unique piece of art, or money stuck between something heavy. Did we have $$$ in our eyes? Our earlier stressed-out feelings were replaced with laughter as we ran back.

It was with eager anticipation that we opened the package. She cut the ribbon while I tore open the paper. You can imagine our surprise and hilarious laughter when we saw what we had found. It was two square plain white colored TILES! One was even chipped in several places. They weren't even hand-painted. Just ugly tiles. They didn't even cushion any large bills. No such luck. So there we were, two very silly feeling runners, laughing aloud at this crazy "gift."

Runners often find odd things or see strange sightings. We certainly think our tiles are quite unique. Not to be forgotten is our famous airplane wing that rests rusting in the Ramapo River. Did Amelia Earhart really fly that far off course? One of these days we'll wade in the water and try to retrieve it.

But that'll be another story . . .

When our run was finished, we learned that, in addition to running, laughter is the best medicine.

On The Run With a Few Good Laughs

It's amazing how often a run can provide us with laughter. This brought back to mind some of my more humorous training runs.

1. It's a long story but one such incident involves a search for a woman's body which I suspected was buried at Rockland Lake by a known serial killer. Foregoing my mentioning of reasons for this conclusion, I'll go on to say that one day I convinced my husband, Roy, to join me in this quest to locate the missing body. It all started when, while doing a nice, leisurely summer run, we ran past "the spot." The light bulb in my head lit up. Publicity about the case had made the local newspapers. I was convinced I was "on to something."

I probably shook Roy's British calm when I suddenly announced, "Let's look for the body. I know it's here somewhere." Although he undoubtedly thought I had lost all my marbles, Roy gamely agreed to help me. So we stopped our run and scrambled through overgrown bushes and maneuvered between trees and rocks. It seemed like such a silly thing to do that in no time at all we were giggling loudly. Bushes rustled as we made our way through this maze. More giggles followed. Shortly thereafter, I found a bone. Could this be it? I must admit to laughing when Roy announced, "Hon, it's only an old soup bone."

Sometime later one of our friends ran by, heard our giggles from the bushes, and loudly proclaimed, "I know what you are doing in the bushes, and it's certainly not running!" How do you explain to someone that you are looking for a woman's body? We sported sheepish grins, laughed some more, and totally convinced the guy that he was right. We knew, however, that the real laugh was on him.

2. A few years ago, a friend and I wanted to mark each mile of our eight mile running route, four miles out and four miles back. It was our mission to measure one mile segments while driving in the car, then jumping out at the precise spot, looking around to make sure no one was watching us, and zapping the road with a spray can of paint. We chose a shocking pink color and painted our measured dots. We laughed at the clandestine nature of our task. The more we sprayed, the more we laughed. We felt so mischievous. Sometimes you just have to be that way.

An occasional car passed and whoever held the spray can quickly put that arm out of sight. Innocent tourists we were! In reality, we were on a runner's mission. How dare anyone interrupt us! With this thought came more laughter.

A year later we went back on the course and while running, we located six of our somewhat faded pink dots. Each sighting was greeted with a hearty "Yes!" and more laughter. Our earlier work was not in vain.

3. Wild turkeys are a sight to be seen by any suburban runner. They exhibit an odd way of walking while bobbing their heads up and down. One such sighting on a winter run really tickled my funny bone.

I came upon six of them crossing the snow-covered backroad just as I approached the bend. Quickly I cut my stride and speed and gingerly crept by. All but one of the wild turkeys made it across the road, this one subsequently scrambling back up the incline.

I waited a while until it decided to make its move. It could not walk down the slippery, icy incline. Instead, it lost its footing and slid down on its backside, legs high in the air. The sight of this creature in such an unnatural position made me laugh. When it finally reached the bottom of the hill it tried to get its balance, only to flop down again. Finally, its feet made contact with the road and it raced across to the other side.

It was then that I saw not six wild turkeys but at least two dozen, some bobbing their heads, some standing still, and others content to slowly walk in the snow.
I thought for a moment that I was taking the RORSCHACH TEST with these funny-shaped black forms against a white, snowy background. Needless to say, I couldn't contain my laughter as I continued on my run.

As you can see there is laughter on the roads. I've certainly enjoyed my share. Hope you have too!

However, there's still the rusty airplane wing in the river on our five mile running route . . .

A Grin, a Smile, a Laugh, and a Klutzenflapper

It was a typical March morning, overcast, windy, a bit muggy, and about 40 degrees. I was into my run, my thoughts, and my peaceful aloneness, contemplating at about the three mile point whether or not to do a hilly eight mile loop. I was happy to be alone in my own little world, grinning as an occasional passing vehicle honked at me.

Looking up at the sky, I smiled as a big bird seemed to be gliding on the thermals above the treetops. It suddenly zoomed downward and made a very hard landing on an upper tree branch. The branch broke off on impact and crashed to the ground while the big bird seemed to be momentarily stunned and suspended in mid-air. A real klutz, I thought! Then its airborne reflexes took over and it flew onto another branch that swayed as it held its weight.

I stopped running and laughed heartily at the sight above me. The bird had a big body and a little head. It did not have the grace or body common to a hawk but seemed to be a turkey buzzard of sorts. After it regained its equilibrium, it just sat motionless on the swaying branch. I stayed for another minute or two just laughing at that klutz of a bird. It was pure laughter for the soul. The rest of my run, even all the many hills, was just so relaxing as I thought about that clumsy bird.

That evening, I related my humorous sighting to my husband Roy. When I couldn't identify the bird, he dubbed it a "klutzenflapper." It is an appropriate name for sure. Since then, during my runs, I keep an eye open for any additional klutzenflappers.

Sometimes a run will bring moments of unexpected laughter just as mine did.

I Am Not Your Dinner (A Running Story)

It was a topsy-turvy kind of running day. The sun couldn't decide whether it wanted to come out from behind the clouds. These same clouds gave way to sporadic snow flurries. I expected to see blue skies to the west and dark, gloomy clouds to the east. Old Man Winter reared its ugly head as the winds gusted at times, then calmed down again. Running was hard and running was easy. An incongruous combination.

As I ran along the roadside, I looked for wildlife activity. Nothing really was stirring this strange February morning. Or so I thought. Occasionally, I noticed movement in the sky. Usually it was a band of noisy crows, making their presence known. However, this was silent but deliberate activity by two hawks, hovering overhead. I noticed that one began flying lower than the other. With each circle above me it swooped lower and lower. I continued running along the lightly traveled roadway, ever mindful of those watchful eyes above me. I saw no recent roadkill, only unrecognizable remnants of an animal long deceased. A few squirrels were active and scurried off as I ran by.

The one bold hawk must have decided that I warranted closer scrutiny. Within a few seconds it appeared to swoop directly down towards my head. I was momentarily paralyzed by fear before my fleet feet took action. I yelled at the hawk, "I am not your dinner!" Scenes from Alfred Hitchcock's film "The Birds" flashed through my mind as I hugged the shoulder of the road.

While still reeling from this perceived "close call," I saw a car coming at me, trying to pass the one in front of it, with a solid yellow line visible. It didn't look like there would be enough room or time for the car to safely re-enter its lane. I envisioned a collision right where I was running. I prepared to jump over the metal guardrail but not in the graceful style of hurdler Gail Devers. Was the driver trying to make roadkill out of me for the brazen hawk? This was way too close for comfort. Luckily, I didn't have to become airborne and leap over the guardrail. I was not destined to be anyone's dinner again. Angrily I raised my fist at the driver.

This was not one's usual running experience. Even though I sometimes think of food when I run, I don't consider myself a candidate for anyone's dinner. I did laugh aloud, however, when I thought about Roy's arrival home from work many hours later and the proverbial question, "What's for dinner?"

Running With Some Flying Friends

It must be that I have a love affair with the bird kingdom when I'm running. Recently, I saw the familiar ugliness of a klutzenflapper, a.k.a. turkey vulture, sitting low on a tree branch along the roadside. It watched me as I ran along this roadway. I stopped running and repeatedly told it how ugly it was, that it was ugliness personified and how could something so ugly keep staring at me. It took off in a huff.

Another time, on that same road, two hawks lazily circled above me, flying lower with each pass-over. The only road-kill nearby consisted of indescribable remnants of a long deceased animal. One hawk flew down so low that I thought it was targeting me for dinner. I flailed my arms wildly while trying to run, mindful that I might become roadkill from a passing, errant vehicle operated by an inattentive driver.

About a year earlier, I saw a large, black object swoop down from the sky above me and clumsily land on a barren tree branch, only to have the branch snap from its weight. The unsuspecting bird, no doubt another klutzenflapper, was temporarily suspended in mid-air. I had to stop running because I was laughing so hard. I called it a dumb bird as I watched it retreat to a more stable structure.

Before that I, by chance, came upon another turkey vulture eating roadkill on the shoulder of the road where I was planting my footstrikes. It was not happy with this meal interruption and came towards me, making loud noises and flapping its wings. I literally flew the coop as my running legs quickly took off.

Of course, there was that time, one winter's day, when I caught sight of a group of wild turkeys crossing the snowy, icy road not too far ahead of me. This humorous sight, described earlier, still brings a smile to my face.

I have tried to outrun guinea hens and sidestep goose droppings. Neither met with much success. In addition I have been hissed at and chased by Canada geese when I have usurped their claimed walking path for my own use.

One very cold winter day, upon a roadside snowbank, I saw a beautiful immobile feathered creature. It was a magnificent small white owl that blended in with the glistening snow. Alas, it was already dead. I felt so sad as I moved it behind the guardrail and marked its resting place with a twig. How and why it got there remains a mystery.

Most recently, as I ran along the tranquil back roads, a lovely bluejay feather came down from out of nowhere. It seemed to gracefully and slowly float downward, nearly missing my nose before landing at my feet. My flying friends always seem to provide me with the impetus to keep running, be it in the bitter cold of winter or the miserable heat of summer. You just never know what wonders of nature will greet you during your runs.

Wrong-Way Abraham at the Reservoir Run

We learned that the roads leading to the Ashokan Field Campus and the five mile course itself had to be changed in a cautionary response to the events of September 11th. As we neared the campus area from the back road we drove past marked miles three and four. We joked about possibly having to run up and down THAT HILL. This was the footplant-test pebble-and-rock-laden dirt road off Beaver Kill Road that led to the parking lot. This was not what I envisioned as being a welcomed part of the new course. Fortunately for one's knees and quads, it wasn't. Yet for Wrong-Way Abraham it was a downhill of knee-killing proportions.

The race director laid out a new and challenging course since we couldn't traverse the reservoir or surrounding roads. It was still a real eye-opener and a hilly one where our leg turnover would be slower. Except for running a dirt road at the beginning and end, this out-and-back course with four hills in each direction (as the race elevation sketch showed) was mostly paved surface. Simple enough to follow, one would think.

However, this was not the case for Wrong-Way Abraham, a.k.a. my husband Roy. A few years ago he took a wrong turn during a grueling race in Wurtsboro. The 11.7 mile run became a half marathon for him and an equally lost soul who eagerly followed him. Prior to that there was Roy's bike race in Flemington, New Jersey. "Let's leave it at that . . .," he said.

Obviously, this is an athlete who finds more challenges and extra miles for himself. Unconventional or creative, one might say. Runner after runner came in. The finish line clock ticked away. Still no sign of Roy. When I asked another runner about him she said, "But he was right behind me." Finally, in the distance and approaching the finish line from the opposite direction, I saw a yellow-jacketed blur with a black-capped head bobbing up and down. Roy took a wrong turn and ran down THAT HILL, giving his sensitive knees infinite reasons to protest. The clock showed a few ticks shy of 52 minutes for Wrong-Way Abraham.

I must admit I really liked the course. Perhaps the next time Wrong-Way Abraham won't live up to his nickname . . . unless, of course, the five mile course changes again.

At the Races with Wrong-Way Abraham

I've written about Roy taking a wrong turn at races. Hence, he earned the nickname Wrong-Way Abraham. Well, it must run in the family because Wrong-Way Abraham II has emerged. That's me.

My off-course adventure occurred at the 10K in Hyde Park, an event I've done several times. I was on a roll, feeling real good and enjoying the race. Until THAT TURN, that is. Road markings were obliterated by weather conditions and sand. With less than one and a half miles to go I overshot the turn. Big time OOPS!

Eventually it occurred to me that I needed to make a turn somewhere. Well, that back road was an endless stretch that went up and down. My sense of humor remained even though my sense of direction failed me miserably. I stopped a car and asked for directions to Route 9G. Onto another hilly road. Going nowhere, I thought. Still, I was enjoying my run and with renewed determination continued to seek out the finish line area. It had to be somewhere. An age group trophy was at stake.

The quiet backroads lifted my spirits. I didn't know where I was nor did I care. I remembered the expression "all roads lead to Rome." Therefore, all roads must eventually take me to the finish line. I looked at my watch. It was now one hour and twelve minutes into the race. No PR (Personal Record) this time. Many footstrikes later I saw houses and asked a man how to get to the high school. He said, "Make a right and another right. It's about a half a mile."

When I reached the main intersection I finally knew where I was. However, I also knew that the school and finish line were still another two and a half miles away. I found a lucky penny by the roadside and continued running. As I approached the side road where the finish line was a vehicle with race officials drove up and offered me a ride back to the school. They said my husband (Roy) was looking for me. I declined because my goal was to run to the finish line and get my time, which I did.

As I proceeded to run back to the school a police car with Roy as the passenger passed me. I again refused a ride back, telling the young officer, "I may be old but I can still run." It was a leisurely run back to the school where a round of applause and a worried husband greeted me. Roy later told me that the Hyde Park Police had put out an All Points Bulletin for me. Gee whiz, I wasn't lost. I just took the road less traveled. My planned 10K turned into an unplanned tour of Hyde Park and an additional six and a half to eight miles. Not too easy for legs that ran a rigorous 30K race a mere week earlier.

This certainly was a memorable experience. I found a total of 13 cents, won my trophy, and earned the right to be called Wrong-Way Abraham II. As for Roy? I came close to giving him an ulcer.

Wrong-Way Abraham Does It Again

It was destined to happen – three strikes for Wrong-Way Abraham. In the 1990s, as described earlier, Roy earned that nickname when he ran off course during the 11.7 mile Roosa Gap race, taking another unknowing runner off the beaten path with him. Both ended up doing a half marathon distance as this wrong turn necessitated much back-tracking. Sometime in the 2000s, he missed the final right turn to the finish during the Mad Dash 10K race. Could the pouring rain have scrambled his brain cells or clouded his vision? This man definitely needs a GPS.

Prior to running the Ed Erichson races (a ten miler and a five miler) this year, we discussed the differences of the two course routes. I bemoaned the double hill trek, whereas he didn't have to do THAT HILL. Although starting later, I caught up to Roy and told him he just passed the three mile marker. Then I continued on my merry way, making that sharp turn onto THAT HILL. After slowly ambling up the hill, I was ever so glad to reach the downhill portion.

After a while, when I was at about the four and a half mile area, a high speed runner appeared, briefly acknowledged me, and was off in a cloud of dust. Always an inspiration to me, he was burning up the asphalt. I was slow as molasses. The asphalt cooled.

Upon completion of our respective races, Roy and I compared notes on the course and who we saw. He said he saw a course marshal stationed at a particular corner, which really puzzled me. He also said that the lead runner passed him sometime before a turn somewhere. Both statements were puzzling because once I saw Roy I never saw him again. I thought we might reconnect later. Then Roy spoke about the hill he climbed. Another puzzlement because the five mile course isn't hilly. I said, "What hill? You had no big hill to tackle." My light bulb lit up when he convinced me he really did see the lead runner and that course marshal. Yes, he really did run up THAT HILL, resulting in a longer than planned five miler.

As previously mentioned, my only wrong-way encounter occurred in Hyde Park when an innocently planned 10K became a 20K when I missed a snow-covered turn arrow. As a result, the wrong-way score stands at Roy three, Erika one. Roy seems to possess this unique ability or affinity to add a long detour during races. I informed him that even though races aren't baseball games, now that he has three strikes, he's out! So folks, give that man a personalized GPS and be on the lookout for Wrong-Way Abraham. He may just challenge your already tired running legs if you follow his lead. Oh yes, if he is telling tall tales when running . . . well, that's another story.

Wrong Way Detour Repeats

What's wrong with adding a few more footstrikes in a race by running the wrong way and going off course? Both Roy and I have gone the wrong way in established races and can still laugh at these unexpected detours and extra mileage.

As previously described, Roy famously ran the wrong way at the Roosa Gap 11.7 mile race and ended up doing a much longer, unplanned distance. Another time he missed the sharp right turn to the finish area, ignoring the within-sight finish line and loud cheering spectators during a Mad Dash 10K race. He eventually got back on track. During one Ed Erichson five mile race, Roy chose to run up the horrible hill instead of following the course's flatter terrain. This extended his distance to a more strenuous six-plus miles instead of his planned five mile trek. Hence, he is forever affectionately dubbed "Wrong-Way Abraham." I even had a commemorative plaque made up in his honor. It has this well-earned moniker painted above a stop watch and a winged running shoe. Very appropriate and now hanging in a revered place of honor in our home.

For me, I once turned a hilly 10K race into a longer unplanned distance run, traversing foreign back roads. A night time snowfall obliterated arrows on the course for the final turn and I just kept going and going and going. Believe it or not, the wonderful finish line crew waited for me to be clocked in. My lengthy detour delayed the awards ceremony until I came bouncing in with a big grin on my face one hour and 56 minutes after I started. I won my age group.

I also ran off course during the 2005 Country Music Marathon. As I traversed the streets of Nashville I was content to be in my own happy little world. While following the runners ahead of me, I turned when most of them did, only to learn that I was now on the half marathon course. I had blithely followed them for about one half mile before realizing my big mistake. Wonders never cease as I finished in 4:56:59 and even managed to win the 65-69 age group award.

Roy and I have taken our off-course blunders in stride. No pun intended. There are bound to be more such detours as we wait with baited breath for our next challenging route change. This affirms the statement that "some mistakes are too much fun to only make once."

Note – some wrong-ways have been described earlier. It's fun to relive them.

Hidden Treasures Abound

I am proof that there are many items to be found on the open roads. My many years' worth of strange stuff picked up give ample testimony to the odd and humorous things one might find. I always look ahead for safe footplants and have found some of the wackiest and worthiest of items.

Some of my strange treasures include: bronze lampshade finial, rawhide dog bone and retractable leash, cassette tape "The Training of a US Marine," wooden handmade dowser stick, one pair of used bicycle pedals, New FELCO Swiss-made clipper tool in a leather case, large bag of Gravy Train dog food (later picked up by car), new unwrapped shower caddy, and a solid ball of multicolored rubber bands. Also, assorted earrings, tools, bungee cords, rolls of miscellaneous tape, baseballs and golf balls, flags, gloves, eyeglasses and sunglasses, toys, head gear, and many loose coins and bills.

Some of the more worthy items include: silver Claddagh necklace and earring set, musical baby's pillow, gold filigree heart pendant, gold wedding band, gold heart and rose pendant, small Limoges vase, metallic magnetic bracelet, digital camera with memory card, man's brown Italian leather wallet containing only $45 in bills, teal and green oval pendant with two silver dolphins on a black cord, and a $100 bill.

One of the silliest things I found by the roadside and ran with was a wrapped new roll of toilet tissue. I hoped no one would stop me and question my decision to carry this on my run. I tried to limit my visibility by running the last three miles of my run on back roads. Once home, I was confronted by Roy's quizzical look and the question, "WHY?"

Car as a Locker Room

Roy and I are an exception to the rule. I call him Mr. Neat. Usage of the words "get organized" from his Air Force service years are high on Roy's vocabulary list. He calls himself Rancid Man, of "It's a bird, it's a plane, it's Rancid Man" notoriety. I am more of a "let's go with the flow" type gal. It seems like a contradiction. Interior vehicle space must be in an orderly, odor-free condition at all times. I am allergic to those aromatic hanging auto deodorizers. Hence, none are used.

Because we do not run long distances anymore, our racing and post-race necessities are minimal now. All race gear is packed in one or occasionally two duffle bags. Other items are small carry-ons, i.e. Gatorade and water bottles, my sugar free Halls cough drops, and Roy's granola bars. If it's hot, Roy's wrung-out T-shirt, along with a small towel, are put into a designated plastic bag on the floor behind the front seats. A damp hat or cap is put on the rear floor mat to air out and dry. There is a plastic bag for empty bottles. Race awards don't smell.

A semi-full quick clothing change is never really necessary. Rancid Man can abdicate his title. I can usually be comfortable continuing to wear race gear home, although a downpour may require some clothing changes and a seat towel. Usually I cover up with my faded red nylon jacket. Mr. Neat requires that military precision order (not odor) be preserved. In reality, we're now primarily a "leave as you came" couple and the car maintains its pristine condition.

Chapter Three - If the Shoe Fits

"It's not important where we are, but it's where we're heading that counts." – Author Unknown

Thoughts on Running

Not too long ago, in one of my pensive moods, I started to think about running, how it all began for me and how much the sport has given me. I thought about all the novice runners who took that same first step on the pavement. It occurred to me that our feelings probably were similar. Whatever our reasons for turning to running were, we must have derived benefits because the sport is still going strong. Runners don't just fade away; they run on and on and on . . .

Whereas many new runners embrace the sport to lose weight, my reason was in response to a challenge from a much younger co-worker. As I'm sure so many new runners have said, I responded to the challenge with, "Why not? What have I got to lose?"

As it turned out, I had nothing to lose but everything to gain. The more I ran, the more I attempted. The more I attempted, the more I succeeded. The more I succeeded, the more I ran. It was an unbroken circle. Running gave me "highs" that I had never experienced before. These were such good feelings.

Novice runners remember many firsts, i.e. the first time they ran a mile . . . or two . . . or three, their first race or first marathon, etc. For me, I was elated when

I initially completed the three mile inner loop course around a nearby lake. I was in seventh heaven! On cloud nine! Soaring like an eagle! How I used to admire those who could run THAT FAR! Now I became one of them. I was a RUNNER!

From these three miles I advanced to six, then nine, and finally to my first half marathon distance. The progression was rapid, resulting in various aches and pains that greeted me all too frequently. Undaunted, I toughened up and ran more. It was an exciting time of my life.

In time familiar faces greeted me as I ran and I felt I was in good company. These were other runners doing what I was doing: running for the love of the sport. The camaraderie at races grew. Runners seem to gravitate towards other runners. My circle of friends became a circle of life. Perhaps that's what running is all about.

Good Bye Sun, Hello Snow

As I am jotting down these thoughts it's a hot, hazy, humid day, one of another long stretch of "triple H" days. My ever-increasing allergies have not been conducive to good, comfortable running this past summer and they are a nuisance today. So it is with great expectation and supreme elation that I start thinking about COLD DAYS, SNOW, AND WINTER! Ahhh ... my sluggish summer legs will then give way to wider strides and quicker hill ascents. Good bye hot sun, hello snow. I'm more than ready!

Being a cold weather person (my description of hot summer runs are "death marches"), I welcome the crisp, clean air of winter, the falling snowflakes, and the beauty of a snow-covered state park. Miserable allergies, seemingly aggravated by anything and everything around, will at last improve to a "comfort zone" state. Already I feel like a wild horse waiting to be tamed by nature's winter surprises. An unexplainable exhilaration seems to take over. The winter air is such a welcomed invitation to run ... and run ... and run. Dehydration worries are tossed by the wayside and sweating doesn't deplete my energy level anymore. Winter running, I love it!

Winter will eventually give way to spring and summer and the emergence of another torrent of allergy miseries. I know that the uphill battles with my allergies will continue but I am determined to forge ahead.

Someone once wrote "Your only limits are those which you set for yourself."

Run a Mile (or Two) in My Shoes

It was a rare balmy (35°F) day sandwiched between the blustery cold days of January. Having left work earlier than usual, I drove to a local state park for a run, aware that many others had the same idea. The parking lot at the fishing station was packed.

The sun peeked sheepishly through a clear sky when I started my quest for a "firehouse seven" or longer run. How refreshing! There were no large areas of ice to gingerly navigate on the inner path. A runner ran by, giving me a familiar "high five" greeting. It was a pleasure to see faces previously shrouded with scarves or balaclavas. Could spring be in the air?

I ran onto the outer south parking lot and up the golf course hill. The large parking lot at the top was still knee-deep in snow, so I ran extra circles around the empty flagpole. While the area around the lake was busy with active runners and walkers, this upper area was devoid of people. Only old windswept footprints on the side snow bank indicated that others had once traversed the area.

My pace down the hill quickened until I reached the outer road again. The rolling hills were kind to my legs this day, prompting me to do intermittent sprints. I made a quick turnaround at the firehouse, then retraced my route back to the starting point. A darkening sky was putting finishing touches to a bright day. It was a GREAT run - one of those rare times when the endorphins kick in and one feels like running forever.

The Fabulous Fifties

Someone once wrote (author unknown) "One of the beautiful things about running is that age has no penalties." So it is with the Fabulous Fifties. In 1991 I celebrated my "reverse 35" birthday. It had been three years since I entered the decade of the fifties. Instead of looking back, I eagerly looked ahead to a new age group in races. Slowing down didn't enter my mind - speeding up did!

Shortly after reaching the half century mark I completed my first triathlon (half mile swim, 16 mile bike, five mile run) and qualified for the New York City Biathlon. Getting bolder in my advancing years, I challenged myself in ultra marathons and a 60K race. The latter was completed in six hours, 22 minutes worth of steady rain.

Since there aren't any limits after reaching age 50, my list of athletic goals still grows in leaps and bounds. If getting there is half the fun, then being there is the pinnacle. As I recently mentioned to Roy, "I've logged a lot of miles on these legs, but honey, you haven't seen anything yet!"

Exceptional Performances

A Speedy 5K - Not usually being a 5K race runner, I found a lot of competitive spirit and some untapped speed when I entered the 5K Winter Series. Running a course (two loops) with a total of four hills (is anything flat in that area?), I was pleasantly surprised when I clocked under 23 minutes for the first two races. This was elation doubled . . . until the third race when very cold temperatures and bitter cold, gusty headwinds did all they could to keep me from moving in a forward direction. With sand blowing in my eyes, headwinds pushing me downhill as I struggled to run uphill and being whipped around like a waywardly tossed football on the open flat areas, I managed to reach the finish line in 23:18. For the final race a smiling sun warmed the runners and I sped to the finish in 22:26, a PR. The races gave me a good winter speed workout and I really had fun doing them.

Medals For Exceptional Performances - A ritual emerged after each race when A-Team partner Roy decided to award us women (myself, a running club member, and a young high school student) "medals for superb performances." You can imagine one guy's chagrin when he heard Roy enthusiastically praising our great performances. He was probably wondering what kind of performances we did! By the way, our "medals" were over-sized chocolate chip cookies.

Seize the Day

I LIKE to run but I don't have to. I HAVE to work but I don't like to. Sound familiar? What this means is that we must often compromise our running, i.e. cutting short our time, decreasing our distance, or rushing to get in "just one more mile."

We battle daylight hours and curse the darkness. We rush to start our run and we rush to get it done. Often our run gets sandwiched in between commitments and responsibilities, job(s) and family, appointments and dinner, etc. We relish the chance to leisurely prepare for our run and to do it with a relaxed mind, without a time table or set distance and with sufficient time to wind down and reflect afterwards. Just for a while I like to say "I don't gotta," meaning that my running time will be something special that I can do just for myself. It's probably the only time that the words "I gotta" bring a big smile to my face.

Not too long ago I met a friend who seemed to be running mega miles every time I saw her. Not having had many opportunities to run, she summed up the situation this way: "Seize the day and make the most of it. That's what I have to do." Even if we are rushing around, short on time, hassled, or whatever, we can still follow her advice and get in quality runs. Just SEIZE THE DAY!

Running for Health

A healthy body has got to belong to a happy person with a relaxed mind. It all fits in. One way to a healthier body is through running. So the theme for this article centers on running for health ... and wealth.

There is no price tag attached to good health. It isn't packaged to be purchased at the store. Yet it is ours virtually free by running. Active, healthy people radiate a special glow. Their eyes shine, they show a sense of well-being, and they possess "that look." Did you ever notice that most women runners aren't afraid to reveal their age or their shape? Okay guys, you look great too!

Running seems to turn back the clock. It invigorates and rejuvenates. It brings on "that look." Age overcomes all boundaries. Both young and old alike share a camaraderie at races. Running makes age insignificant. It's that simple. So run and be healthy. You'll get wealthy in ways that money can't buy.

Not Speeding Ahead

Gandhi once said, "There is more to life than increasing its speed." I will apply these words to age-related slowness in running. Yes, the years whiz by all too quickly, even if one is always "on the go." As my age goes up, so do my racing times. Now pulling 77 and pushing 78, I am content to travel in the slower lanes of life while slowly but surely still moving forward. It's amazing how losing one's racing speed creeps up, seemingly gradual at first, then more pronounced. Longer race distances are relegated to the back burner. Reaching the finish line at the onset of darkness is not appealing. Big time rebelling knees and sore, aged bones are not welcome.

It's been hard for me to reflect on the "good old days" when I see my finish line times go sky high. Creaky bones and tired muscles don't move as fast. Wishing won't make it so. It's akin to slamming one door shut while slowly opening another, a crack at a time. Once I reveled in my 21-22 minute 5Ks, then 25 minutes, then, oh Lord!, 30 minutes. Slowness personified. Now, it's usually in the 36- minute range, occasionally less . . . if I am lucky. My pace is akin to "shuffling off to Buffalo." Hey, there is humor in all aspects of one's running life.

My goal is to keep on keepin' on. This will be in direct conflict with my orthopedic doctor's edict: "No more running, Erika." However, it is in being true to that nagging inner voice that keeps whispering, "GO FOR IT." I will strive to be persistent, patient, and happy just to be a race finisher. Thus, I will embrace my age-related slowness while sporting a grin that is far bigger than my stride. So be it.

Chapter Four - Footsteps in Double Time

"The road to success is dotted with many tempting parking spaces." – Author Unknown

Brrr . . . It's Cold Outside

It was all Roy's idea. Get up early, brave the elements, and do a hilly 8.6 mile run in preparation for an upcoming 10 mile race. However, when the alarm went off at 5 AM we could only moan and groan "Oh, no, not already. It's much too early." After quite a few extra lazy minutes our conscience got the best of us. However, we did not make a hasty exit out the door but fiddled and faddled until nearly 6:30 AM. Our adventurous feline, Brooks, wanted to run out the door more than we did.

Boy, was it cold! The TV reported three degrees for a nearby city and it certainly was no warmer in our town. We decided to tackle the course in opposite directions, parting at the traffic circle in town and meeting somewhere near the mid-point. I like to run up the long steep hill while Roy prefers to punish his knees by running down it. The wind was acceptable but reared its ugly head on the hilly back roads. Peaceful, not much traffic, and so very cold! My polio legs were reluctant to move in the chilly air so I plodded along. At age 10 I contracted non-paralytic polio. Many years later I experienced legs that often were reluctant to move forward, due to the onset of a mild form of Post Polio Syndrome in my early sixties.

We passed each other on THAT HILL, pausing only long enough to exchange a quick "hi" and an even quicker "good bye, see you at the home front." It certainly was an interesting run to talk about. Roy saw more than two dozen large wild turkeys who raced off when he neared their spot. His bottle of water froze and the Power Bar in his pocket took on the hardness of a gold brick from Fort Knox. Roy said that when a truck passed him a second time the driver yelled, "Didn't I see you an hour ago?" to which Roy replied "I'm a glutton for punishment." Roy said it gave him a moment to chuckle before continuing his run.

I had my own adventure, having found an air gun (minus its CO2 cartridge) lying alongside the road. Of course, I couldn't leave it there so I carried it in my left hand while running the last five miles. How can one hide a large, heavy gun like that? I hoped no one would see it by my side and call the police. I envisioned being arrested. Although I wore warm gloves the metal chilled and numbed my fingers. Still, I tried not to be too obvious with what I was carrying (the gun was later turned over to the local police). I don't normally carry water on very cold days but do try to keep my trusty Power Bar in chewable condition by holding it in my hand. To take periodic bites I had to put the gun down and remove my gloves.

Cold weather running can be challenging and, if one is lucky, can provide unexpected sights and findings. This run was exhilarating for both of us. We just couldn't wait to get back home and savor a cup of hot coffee.

A Cold Weather Runner

I am a bona fide cold weather runner. When others utter, "BRRRRR . . . it's cold outside," I say to myself, "Bring it on." Particularly for me is the joy of running in the pristine snow where my footprints are the only visible signs of the road being traversed. The sun glistens on the new fallen snow as it peeks through the leafless, snow-covered tree branches. A lonely woodpecker can be heard in the distance. I pause to survey deer and rabbit tracks along and across the road. Sometimes I am lucky to catch a fleeting glimpse of one or the other. An air of tranquility prevails.

As the snow continues to fall, I am encrusted in a white cover, the sole movements of a creature akin to the Abominable Snowman of folklore. I listen to my slow moving feet as the snow crunches beneath my running shoes with every footstrike. The cold, brisk air soothes an inflamed knee. I am comfortable and pain free . . . and slow. Running in the snow is more tiring and energy-consuming. I am content with the pace and my aging body does not rebel. All is good.

The heat and humidity are the wrath of summer running for me. Now, I am in no hurry to end my run. Quite a contrast to the "I'm dragging my feet" times on hot, hazy, and humid summer runs when I can't wait to proclaim, "I've had it for today." In the winter the scorching sun does not bake me like a reddened lobster. Rather, it has a wonderful warming effect and I now welcome its presence.

I have fond memories of completing several 50K races where the park roads were icy and traversing them took cautionary measures and short strides. I was in my glory then as I counted each hard-trekked loop and was enthusiastically greeted by other runners at the finish. Although my damaged knee now limits these long distances, I can still recall how joyous I felt on those winter days as I conquered the cold, the miles, and the slippery terrain. I can't find this unrestrained joy in the hot, humid, and hazy days of summer where I readily become a wilted rose. I need the cold, the snow, and the tranquility of my winter runs.

As a side note, I recently ran on the coldest day in decades in early January. With the wind chill, it was about minus 20 degrees as I braved all the elements for my 3.6 mile run. Roy went to the warm indoor gym. He told the gym personnel that he was sending the men in white coats with their butterfly nets out to rein me in. They could not catch me that day.

A Christmas Day Run

Terry Anderson, former hostage in Beirut, once said, "Running is peace and quiet and freedom." These words echoed my feelings when I did a late morning run on Christmas Day.

As I ran through our town's Main Street area, I admired the colorful holiday decorations, enjoyed the tranquility from the absence of vehicles and pedestrian traffic, and was at peace with my surroundings. I could run wherever my feet took me. I glanced at the local pet grooming store's wide picture window and caught a glimpse of a beautiful calico cat which was snoozing inside and basking in the sun's warm rays.

About a mile down, the road intersected with a main road. I marveled at how devoid of vehicles this normally high traffic road was. It added to the serenity of my run. The roadside shoulder was clear of earlier ice and snow conditions. The trees were eerily bare and crackled in the breeze. I welcomed the sun's warmth on my face and the partially cloudless sky. I traversed a small bridge over the fast-flowing nearby creek and viewed a small waterfall. How peaceful it all was.

The temperature hovered around 30 degrees and sometimes the sun played hide and seek with the clouds. The air felt colder then and I ran faster to keep warm. I passed a new development being constructed with mega McMansions encroaching on what was once solely wildlife territory. I retraced my steps back into town. A few wayward carts were in the shopping plaza and I brought them closer to the supermarket. I must have looked really funny pushing shopping carts while running in the empty parking lot. I missed the pleasant aroma of coffee from the closed Dunkin' Donuts store. Actually I yearned for a hot cup of java. The same cat was still in the pet grooming store's window. This time I stopped and tapped on the glass. It stirred and stretched and looked at me with half-closed eyes. A dog inside barked. Time to get my feet moving in a forward direction again and head for home.

Total mileage: 5.8 miles
Money found: 36 cents
This run: Priceless.

The Snow Elephant

The snow elephant. That's what I felt like when I bundled up in layers of clothing for a winter run in the snow. The previous day's storm had blanketed the area with more than a foot of heavy, wet packed snow. The next day winds whipping around with hurricane force gusts made the outdoor temperature feel even colder. As I prepared for my run, the wind chill factor was definitely something to consider. My multi-layered garments soon made me feel like an over-stuffed elephant.

I gingerly set out on my run, ever aware of deceptive patches of black ice. There was much snow covering the sidewalks and roads. Flakes were being blown upward from the trees and the roadside drifts. Brrrrrr . . . did this runner shiver!

My planned running route was a six to seven mile course encompassing many back roads. As I exited from my apartment complex's main driveway, the strong winds buffeted me on the downward portion of the roadway. My attempts to utilize the sidewalks along the main thoroughfare soon proved futile. So deep was the snow that I felt like an elephant slowly plodding along.

Shortly thereafter, while running along the hilly section of backroads, I came upon a walker, briskly stepping through his paces. As we briefly strode side by side I commented, "Boy, this is tough going." The walker concurred with, "Yeah it sure is!"

It was a severe winter wonderland along the stretch of road known as Boulevard and I quickly became engrossed in the beauty surrounding me. Snow-laden branches creaking and bending in the breeze, glistening snow-covered woods shimmering brightly from bits of the sun's rays, and the bright blue sky framing it all.

A bitter cold crosswind tossed me around like a misguided puppet on a string as I neared the end of Boulevard. A short time later another forceful gust of wind pushed me backwards while I vainly tried to run in a forward direction. Even running downhill took a lot of effort. My legs were already so tired that lifting them in the snow became harder with each footstep.

I approached the scenic upper area with many sharp turns and short streets with a real slow gait. Nearby wind chimes melodically swayed in the breeze. I was engrossed in the beauty of the Hudson River and Storm King Mountain when I approached a man diligently shoveling snow off his roadside parked car. The road was narrow and his vigorous arm movements thrust the shovel's long handle outward. As I cautiously proceeded to pass him I yelled "runner to your right." He was quite startled to see me and apologetically stopped shoveling to let me pass. Nice gesture. I thanked him.

So many drivers slowed down when they passed me on the snowy road. No one blew a horn to startle me. Perhaps the season's first big snowstorm mellowed everyone.

The sidewalks along the east side of town were partially clear but slippery in spots, therefore I again chose to run on the roadway where specks of wet pavement peeked through. This seemed less risky. A runner with a faster pace came from behind me and passed me. My energy level did not match his. Soon this runner turned around to retrace his steps and I saw the word "ARMY" emblazoned on his grey sweatshirt. Hmmmm, a cadet from nearby West Point, I wondered.

At the next intersection a women driver patiently waited for me to cross the road. I waved to her and mouthed a smiling "thank you." Again the roads were better to traverse than the sidewalks.

The next uphill portion of the course was energy-draining and I had to force my tired legs to push forward with all their might. I was mindful of having no shoulder to run on as well as road traffic splashing me with slush. However, drivers again slowed and drove with caution as they passed me. They probably thought, "What is this crazy woman doing running in the snow on a day like today?"

The hardest part of my run was going up the final long hill. This three quarter mile stretch is always a good workout. Today it sapped whatever bit of energy I had left. The road surface was slippery, slushy, and snow-covered with few visible bare spots. Trudging uphill in this mess drained the starch from me. The accompanying winds greeted me with repeated forceful gusts. Moving my arms faster didn't help. My feet and legs were simply too tired to "put on the speed."

Snow running is exhilarating, fun, challenging, and tiring. It takes a lot more effort to run in the snow. The legs don't move as fluidly, giant-sized strides are non-existent, and, when confronted with gale force winds, it becomes nearly impossible.

However, in the final analysis, being a snow elephant did have its own special moments for me. A part of me didn't want the run to end, yet the desire for a warm home overpowered me. I called it quits, unlocked the door, and welcomed the warm inside temperature . . . and a hot cup of coffee!!!

This snow elephant had come home to stay!!!

Snowstorm Running

I am a cold-weather person, preferring to run in the winter months, rather than during the "dog days of summer." Hot sun and relentless humidity are a real turn-off. Crunchy snow soothes my feet and bad knees better than any beach sand. Bring on the snow, and the kid in me comes to life. So, with wide open arms, I welcomed our first recent big snowfall, the proclaimed "Blizzard of 2016." Well, the projected blizzard fizzled in our area, bringing very strong winds but only about five inches of snow.

Shortly after the first flakes hit the ground, I got ready to tackle my planned morning run. The cold, blustery winds were whipping up fiercely, and a light snow quickly blanketed the streets. Blowing snow hit me in the face like sharp pellets, and the relentless strong headwinds blew me in all directions. The falling snow was not my only foe as the winds turned me into a tumbleweed, akin to scenes from the Dust Bowl areas out west. Only this time, it was from the overpowering blowing snow. I could not believe how quickly the snow accumulated, making each footstrike a tenuous one. Moving forward was, at times, a daunting task. Traffic was nearly nonexistent and the serene beauty of Mother Nature was everywhere. As the visibility worsened, my wool hat was pulled down to my eyebrows, and I peeked out from under its brim.

Of course, I was not the only fearless runner battling the elements. Roy went out in the opposite direction, and we met on a local side street. We were so bundled up that I commented that we looked like the oversized "Michelin Tire Man" minus the rolls of blubber. Many

of the stores in our shopping plaza had not yet opened, and an eerie stillness permeated the nearly empty parking lots.
My search there for loose coins was futile.

While my bad knees rebelled in the cold, the child in me reigned supreme.

Total miles: 3.9
Meeting Roy: A pleasant diversion
Letting the child in me emerge: Priceless

Chapter Five - Missteps (Or Missed Steps)

*"Because some runs are not about the finish line." –
Author Unknown*

Down and Out and Going Nowhere

Yep, that's what I was - down-hearted, down-trodden, and out of the running scene. Grounded.

Like a few diehards, the bitter cold, snowy days of January had not deterred me. Like them, I ran on icy, snow-covered roads, leaped over high mounds of snow, breathed in the crisp cold air, and ran and ran and ran.

The end came rather abruptly during a 10K race in late January when a ruptured plantar fascia jolted me out of commission. With crutches, a soft cast, and a huge ugly bootie for my foot, I quickly lost all my athletic movements as a runner. It was "Oh, darn %#*!!!," followed by the "Oh woe is me" syndrome. All I could think about was NOT RUNNING! In rapid time I was climbing the walls.

Aaron Neville may croon, "Don't take away my heaven." Well, that's how I felt knowing that the Boston Marathon was looming somewhere in the near future. Running was my heaven; now it was taken away.

My first attempts at running brought too much pain and I had to scratch that premature plan. Forget about walking. Runners' feet are not made for walking and I was no exception. I wanted to travel in the fast lane! Being at a local lake, where runners abounded, didn't offer me any incentive to go to a lower gear and walk.

In due time I tried roller skating, but it was not the same. I was still THINKING RUNNING! No matter what I was doing, the urge to go for a run was always there.

Then one day in early March another snowfall cushioned the pavement. My good intentions to walk fell by the wayside. Slowly, ever so slowly, I guided my legs with a running motion. It must have looked like I was doing a poor imitation of a Charlie Chaplin routine. One foot, then another foot, then another . . . I was actually running!

Preferring to run long distances, I surprised myself at running a mere 2.3 miles. I felt like the comeback kid. Runners have to run. That's all there is to it.

As I write this, it's 42 days 'til Boston. I may not run well against the five-hour clock limit, but I will run the marathon.

A Dangerous Trio

A dangerous trio: dizziness, disorientation, and dehydration. Now that the heat and humidity are upon us, I thought I'd write about a recent frightening experience. It should serve as a warning to all runners: beware of running in the hot weather. Take precautions.

The temperature was already in the 70s when the start of the 10K race was delayed for 15-20 minutes. I recall feeling very warm as I stood among 7,000 other women participants in the hot sun for the start of the Advil Mini Marathon. Yet, despite the heat, I felt good. A daily dose of a prescribed antihistamine had finally brought my earlier allergy-related breathing and running discomforts to an acceptable range. My little bottle of water-Gatorade mixture was clutched tightly in hand. I didn't want to drink any of it, lest I deplete my supply before the race began.

For the first four miles I ran well and tried to ignore the heat. With split times of 6:45, 14:02, 21:11 and 28:22, I was running for a PR. Then it happened . . .

I remember stopping short in my tracks, with legs that didn't want to move and feeling dizzy and disoriented. This sudden onset of symptoms caught me by surprise. I tried to focus on forging ahead but everything around me was spinning, even when I tried walking. When I finally regained some equilibrium, I clumsily tried to resume running. Several runners offered assistance but I waved them away with, "Thanks, but I am going to try to finish."

As soon as I reached the finish line chutes (time 49:09), two members of the medical team grabbed me. Someone removed my bib tag. I remember being helped to a cot, lying down, and being soothingly cooled with ice packs and water. These medical personnel were wonderful in the care and concern they administered to me. They got me back on wobbly feet, reminding me to keep drinking lots of water. For many hours thereafter, I experienced nausea and headache pain.

What shocked me the most about this incident was the sudden onset of symptoms. True, I felt thirsty while running, but I thought I had consumed enough fluids. The fact that I was running well made me bypass two water stations for a "quick sip from my bottle." Not a wise decision.

Dehydration is deceptively insidious in creeping up on a runner. Please learn from my experience. Remember to hydrate well.

When the Going Gets Tough

You want to run hard, the conditions are ideal and your heart says you have a good race coming up. The starting gun goes off and you make a mad dash to "find your spot" among the runners. You tackle the first three flat miles with some gusto, even though you're not feeling quite up to par. It's that same old tired feeling creeping in. It seems to be your constant running buddy these days. You ignore it, hoping it will go away. Then come the dreaded hills. You see them in the distance. Are they for real, you wonder? The road under your feet gets steeper and you start to tilt. They are for real! You give it all you've got only to discover you've got nothing! You just can't go on, you have to start walking.

When a small, short crest appears you begin to run again only to face another hill . . . and another. More walking gets you through. Somehow you conquer all the uphills and start to appreciate the splendid downhills. Yet the energy needed to really forge ahead never materializes. Even on the flats it seems like you're dragging. Before you can reach the finish line another hill greets you, followed by several "speed bumps" that feel like more hills. As you struggle to finish an over-whelming tiredness takes over. In what seems like endless minutes, you finally make it! The clock shows 1:11:38.

I have just taken you through a 15K race (9.3 miles) which I ran in mid-March, and after I learned that I had an iron deficiency problem. It really was "tough going" for me.

A Reverse Perspective

Black ice in our parking lot - that was my undoing on the morning of the last Winter Series 5K race. Black ice was there and so was I!!! The end result was a fall resulting in painful abrasions and bruises to my left leg. The small hole at the knee in my lycra tights did not indicate the extent of the injured area. By the time I arrived at the race site, the aspirin had eased the pain a bit. Yet I knew that I couldn't competitively run the race.

Already having three good races behind me, I decided to test the injured leg by running the course in reverse at a much slower pace. Thus began my reverse perspective. My familiarity with the course was no longer there, snow covered any significant landmarks and I got confused with a number of turns. Everything looked different!

By taking the reverse route I got to see a different perspective of the runners. No longer was I blindly following someone's back; I actually saw faces! Also, I got to see the lead runners and marveled at how easy they made uphill running appear. The fluid strides of the lead runner amazed me.

As I ran down the hills into the wind the others ran up with the strong wind propelling them along. It felt strange for me to run in a clockwise direction. Yet it felt even stranger for me not to be competing with the other runners. My reverse perspective left me with a feeling of loneliness.

Putting on the Brakes

It was Mother's Day 1993 and my heart was geared up to run a half marathon. On this particular Sunday a nagging sore throat and cough persisted, so I did what I usually, albeit often unwisely, do: I chose to ignore these symptoms.

When the race started I "flew with the flow," reaching the one mile mark at my usual sub-seven-minute pace. My legs felt good and strong but my chest and breathing felt the opposite, like I was slowly being mowed over by a Mack truck. The more I ran the drier and more sore my throat felt. I thought my chest was being sawed with a serrated knife and my lungs compressed in a vise with each breath.

At two miles my legs and heart were still on a roll but the rest of me wasn't. At three miles, fearing a strep infection, I finally knew I was too sick to continue. The race would go on without me. Sadly I dropped out and started walking back to the start. I had to chuckle when several bystanders along the way asked me if I was the lead runner. Imagine the lead runner walking! It was really quite comical.

Roy often says that I know only two speeds: fast and stop. Well, this time I had to put on the brakes and stop racing for that day.

Straying off the Beaten Path

It's not a New Year's resolution already broken. It's a new year and a time to begin anew. It's a new time to think about gearing your running to the beat of a different drummer. In a nutshell, dare to make changes in your running/training program. Dare to slow down a bit and smell more flowers; dare to take off a day or two to rest. Ponder about your real motives for running. Are they set to a rigid pattern or is running for the fun of it a part of your training? Change your rigid running patterns/routine to stop, rest, relax, regroup and recuperate.

A major change for me was to lay off from running. This wasn't by choice as it should have been. It was dictated to me by a very sick body. I did not voluntarily take off eight straight days to give pavement pounding a rest. I had no choice – a flu/gastrointestinal virus was the culprit (or blessing).

Things just didn't go right on my last training run. Attending to pre-holiday preparations and an extra busy job schedule were exhausting to the core. On my last six and a half mile run, the hills were not welcomed challenges but became unwanted curses because my legs did not want to move forward or upward. How I wished I could have chosen to avoid them on my planned running route! I had no energy to propel my legs in a moving manner. Instead, they felt glued to the pavement. In hindsight, I should have known that something was amiss.

Symptoms of lethargy and cramps were followed by fever, chills, loss of appetite, and other discomforts.

Still, my mind couldn't conceive the notion that the body could not run.

I tried in vain to keep my running schedule. Faithfully I'd assemble all my running gear. Psychologically, I guess I thought the mind would win over the body's refusal to move. However, it became harder and harder to get out of bed. I slept so much that I thought I'd shatter Rip Van Winkle's record! I became an expert at making a beeline dive from the bedroom to the bathroom. This was the extent of my "running." Sadly, all the running gear was left untouched.

After eight days of this nonsense, I felt I'd had enough. So, on the ninth day, I ran. Ahhh, the exhilaration of speed! It was a wonderful run in the cool, crisp winter air. The hills were minor rumbles along the way. I felt energetic and rejuvenated. What a great run!

Did I learn that straying off the beaten path and altering one's running patterns to allow for rest was necessary? Obviously not, because the impulsive runner in me again did too much too soon, and I'm back to square one with a bad cold and aching body.

Today I am resting. The tomorrows will now be tackled one day at a time. I have vowed not to dare to stray off the beaten path and "give running a rest." The New Year is young and I am persistent (or stubborn, as my father would say) . . . so, we'll see.

Toe-ing the Line

The BIG TOE - only when it is injured do we realize how important it is to ourselves as runners. I know because I was hurting.

My problem originated as a blackened toenail on my big toe that was compounded by repeated poundings and pressure to it. Using the "band-aid approach" and not much common sense, I could get through races and even completed the Boston Marathon. Of course aspirins were a necessity, downhills were cursed, and uphills were blessed. Well, perhaps I cursed the uphills a bit also.

Yet the toe's pain worsened while the nail continued to take on a grotesque appearance. I covered it with a sock and tried to ignore it, an approach that proved to be no good in the long run. A friend recommended that I see her mother's podiatrist. But her mother is a number of years my senior and is not a runner!

Runners are a different breed. We don't want to be told that we cannot run. While I agonized over this decision my toe was in agony with pain. However, the bottom line was that I did not want to be told that I could not run.

As the nail became more ugly and the pain grew more intense, I grew more fearful. I wanted to be put out of my misery, not out of commission. Then, as fate would dictate, my big toe met its Waterloo during a long 21 mile training run. After completing the first flat six miles (a double inner loop around the lake), I knew that I was headed for trouble - big time pain! By the time I started my final stretch of six miles, I knew it would be a battle of pain. Being off-balance because I couldn't put much weight on my foot, off-stride because I tried to compensate for this, and too stubborn to call it quits, I hobbled in on the final one mile straightaway road. Tears fell like Niagara Falls on my cheeks. I was in pain! It was time for medical action, not running.

Being chicken to the core, I chose a podiatrist who was also an athlete and decided to try his "progressive foot care" approach. In no time at all the nail pressure on the toe and the fluid build-up under the nail were alleviated. The professional medical treatment performed gave me the most relief I had had in months. In fact, I tried out my "new" big toe the next day by running a good-paced twelve and a half miles, encompassing hills and valleys around the lake.

Hello heaven, good bye hell. I was running pain free and loving every minute of it.

Short on Memory - Long on Spirit

For many runners participating in a challenging or competitive race or event, these words are often muttered before, during, or after the event: "Never again!" These two innocuous words pack a wallop when first said, yet their impact is short-lived. Runners quickly forget.

An example of runners not having an elephant's memory (you know, an elephant never forgets) is during marathons, races, or other endurance events. A hard course to traverse, unforgiving hills, a bad start, lack of cooperation from Mother Nature, poor performance, a hamstring pull, tough going when the going got tougher - all these and more can trigger the "Never again!" response. Still, there is a yearning to go back and face the challenge again.

Because of their relentless and constant strain on the human body, marathons are the target of so many "Never again!" resolutions. The 1994 inaugural Warwick Marathon was known for its tough hills after the fact. Many runners cursed the unforgiving hills with moans, groans and resolves of "Never again!" Some probably meant it, while others spoke out of exhaustion upon the completion of this difficult course. The Boston Marathon, with its many undulating hills, the late-coming Newton Hills and the notorious Heartbreak Hill, is a great example of one saying "Never again!" However, the urge to "come back and conquer" doesn't die.

Another kind of "Never again!" is often said after one is injured while participating in a sport. The words originate out of fear of having that same injury or fall occur. For example, a bicycle fall or accident can prompt the rider to never again want to ride. The fear may not vanish, but it is later masked by the athlete's competitive spirit and drive . . . or just plain love of the sport. Thoughts like these occur: "Gee, if I could finish the biathlon, I may be able to try a triathlon next time." Or, "I really want to go out on my bike today."

Soon the bike gets dusted off, memory fades, injuries heal, and a spirit of "just do it" takes over. Doing training rides over the area where the accident/fall occurred soon increase the rider's confidence. "Never again!" is replaced with "Oh, what the heck, I can do it."

Often the words "Never again!" act as a catalyst to get us "back on track" with our lives. To say "never" towards something seems to reach the core of an athlete's being. It is often a challenge reborn, an urge to go for it, an itch that must be scratched. "If I tried it once, I can try it again." The spirit begins to soar. A job unfinished needs to be tackled. The athlete becomes short on memory but long on spirit and plots the next move . . .

The words "Never again!" just don't warrant merit. The spirit takes over, everything else is forgotten, and the challenge is met. In the final analysis, you can break the body, but you can't break the spirit.

One More for the Road

When someone really enjoys running it is so easy to write about one's adventures on the roads. Most of my own ideas for running related articles are drawn on personal experiences. Often these experiences can better be termed trials and errors. My recent road running mishaps form the basis for this article. I hope all readers who run can relate to it.

It had been about two and a half weeks since my untimely fall on the trail at the Roosa Gap 11.7 mile Roller Coaster Run. There my left leg made contact with the terra firma first, followed by a hard roll onto my right side and hip. Not being one to worry, I quickly got up, limped a bit, and gamely continued to run the more than nine miles left to go. It was not the kind of roll I wanted to be on! I ached.

When I reached the finish line I may have looked battered and bruised but only a fellow runner could understand and appreciate the smile on my face. The job was done. More training days were ahead. No time to be down and out from running.

The training run in question was actually preceded two days earlier, except weather conditions were different. However, as Murphy's Law would dictate, both shared similar fateful endings.

On the earlier run, as only a compulsive runner can do, I took to the roads, happy to enjoy the crisp autumn temperature and the peacefulness of the hilly back roads. I looked for deer but did not see any this time. I suspect they may have been watching me from afar as

I invaded their territory. "Boy, it feels to good to run!" I thought to myself over and over again.

Enter Murphy's Law #101: If an object to trip on is in the road, it will occupy the same spot where the runner's foot is planted. Or better yet, it's when the left foot doesn't know what the right foot is doing. It makes you wonder how you can trip over something other than your own two feet. Believe me, this takes talent. Lots of talent!

Well, in a flash I lost my balance, managed to avoid knee and body contact with the pavement, but twisted my left ankle like a pretzel. Sore and feeling rather stupid, I limped home. Good intentions of icing the injury never materialized. Big mistake.

The error of my ways became apparent during the next day's run. Of course I was going to do my training run with a "business as usual" attitude. Likewise, I chose to ignore the tenderness in the ankle and even did the quarter mile sprint after my long run. Am I a slow learner or what?

The following day the skies opened up with a torrential rainfall accompanied by strong, gusty winds. To run or not to run? That was the question that again faced me. Should I risk further injury to the ankle to run in the pollen-free air? Yes!!! It was good breathing weather and would afford me the opportunity to run free of allergy discomforts. My husband advised me to "think about it." I did, then after a fleeting thought, I was out the door . . .

The rain subsided only briefly, then hit me with full force. The headwinds roared fiercely, menacingly blowing the tree branches. Still, I felt compelled to complete my planned seven mile run. Compulsive, obsessive behavior? You bet!

Fallen branches and debris littered the back roads. Occasionally I bent down to remove twigs and junk from the road. The usual deer seen on this route again remained out of sight. Were they wiser than this runner?

Midway through my run a truck pulled alongside me and the driver asked, "Can I give you a ride outta the rain?" "Oh no, this is beautiful," I replied, "Thank you anyway." I suspect he was shaking his head in bewilderment as he drove away. As for me, I was drenched. How much wetter could I get?

More gusty winds and relentless raindrops greeted me. It was one downpour after another. I was alone on the roads. When I reached the main section of town it too was devoid of people outside. Me? I just kept sloshing along, enjoying my own private world as a runner.

The winds buffeted me as I ran uphill and blew me along on the downward portions. Soon home was in sight. I was extra cautious as I approached the gravel-laden area where I had previously twisted my ankle. How fast can one really run in a downpour?

As fate beckoned, "it" was there awaiting my unsuspecting arrival. The "it" was a big water main hole in the road with the cover being several inches below the resurfaced pavement. Leaves and darkened water disguised the hole. It caught my left foot, twisted it painfully, and forced me to land hard on the rain-soaked pavement. A neighbor who saw me fall offered assistance. How nice it was that strangers still cared.

I had gotten in my run, my "one more for the road" run. However, I had not bargained for the painful consequences.

About a week later I learned that I was not alone in suffering from a twisted ankle. Another local runner met the same fate. However, he had the presence of mind to quickly put his injured foot in a nearby stream. He related that he was up and running the next day while I was grounded and relegated to exercising on the stationary bike for a week.

The moral? Enjoy your running and do your "one more for the road" run with caution, especially if Mother Nature wields her nastiness on you.

A View from the Back of the Pack

It was not a time for me to race. Running at a slower pace was a questionable and untested option. Rather, I had planned to "bring up the rear" (literally!) at a 4.4 mile run by moving forward in some manner of fashion with Roy at my side.

A freak accident 16 days earlier sent me smashing to the ground with the coccyx area and left leg taking the brunt of the fall off a step-stool. I saw stars and everything else. A mega pain to contend with. Forget about walking comfortably. Dismiss any thoughts of running. Lament over the pain. Most distressing was the thought of not being a supporting participant at this annual race.

My spirits were buoyed when X-rays showed no pelvic or lumbar fractures. It was time to think positive and join Roy for this run . . . maybe! To combat the pain I experimented with how to regulate and time Tylenol doses for maximum pain relief so I could move forward and faster with each step.

Race day brought a near-perfect day weather-wise along with the most participants to date. I could not do a warm-up run for fear of exacerbating the pain. So minimal quasi-stretches sufficed. Roy and I started and ran together, albeit slowly, and truly enjoyed ourselves and the course.

Since a winning time was never a viable thought, I could enjoy just being there and watching the field of runners ahead of me. I saw the race from a different perspective and thought of how it felt to be the caboose. It would be a thrill to merely reach the finish line this day.

Gingerly I followed the footsteps of a friend with the determined spirit of a veteran runner, but my injured area hurt. OUCH!

Then something unique happened. With about a mile to go I felt like I was floating on air. That my feet were not even touching the pavement. That I had wings and was flying. That the mind dulled all the earlier pain. It produced an incredible adrenaline high for me. Unfortunately, a side stitch gave Roy an adrenaline low. We separated. I had to keep moving. The fear of the unknown kept me cautious in my earlier movements until that adrenaline high lifted me beyond my wildest expectations.

I have to thank the young woman who stood near the top of the last short uphill trek and cheerfully greeted all incoming runners. Her words of encouragement were music to one's ears.

This race is wonderfully challenging. The downhills later on are worth it after running up that one long hill at the beginning. I really enjoyed my run and the view from the back of the pack.

A Change of Pace

Since early February 2006 I had endured so much down time from running. Being an avid runner, it became a case of doing too much too soon more times than I cared to think about. When it came to running I was an incorrigible addict who listened to her heart and I enjoyed being on the open roads. In time I realized that certain pains could not be eternally ignored. The sage advice of my podiatrist, "You have to listen to your body, Erika," were words that finally sunk in.

After another layoff, seven weeks this time, I felt recovered enough from a nagging foot injury to run the new Three Seasons Challenge, a low-key three mile event. Although my ailing foot was not really in synch with this, I was psyched up, pumped up, and ready to make tracks. I finished in 27:55 and was smiling from ear to ear.

A 10 miler beckoned a week later and I listened to my body. Well, sort of, because part of me was listening to my heart. The race started, a bottle fell out of my fuel belt with my first step forward, and I then stood there until I could safely pick it up. Oh, the joy of running! Speed was not part of the equation for me. Rather, fun and finishing were paramount. As I ran, I was listening to my injured foot touching the pavement and going at an easy change of pace.

About three miles into the race, I saw a nickel and a shining good luck penny on the roadside, which I just had to pick up. This was followed by a lot of pennies, nickels, dimes, and quarters strewn along a quarter mile stretch of the roadway. Every time I started to run again there was more money!! Loose change was everywhere. Two bottles fell out of my fuel belt as I bent down and I had to go back and retrieve them. Runners passed me. Time went by the wayside as the loose coins continued to materialize and I kept picking them all up. The change of pace cost me about six to seven minutes. At the water station at 4.7 miles I handed my heavy coin-laden wristband to a wonderful, understanding volunteer who promised she would bring it to the finish line area, which she later did. Feeling light in spirit because of being able to run, I ambled onward. The miles added up and soon the park entrance came into view. My clock time was slow, my heart was beating with joy, and my foot was throbbing. All total, I found $3.12 3/4 (one penny had a quarter sliced off), and my foot held up better than expected.

Roy also found some humor on the course. A red pickup trucked pulled alongside him at about mile nine and the driver said, "Hang in there," to which Roy replied, "Give me a rope!" Roy gave it a kick at the finish line.

As a side note, I probably should have iced the foot afterwards. However, it was the day before my 68th birthday and, being half of a Dynamic Twin Duo, Roy and I had plans to visit my twin sister to celebrate our mutual big day. Call it a change of pace, because eating the icing on the cake was the only icing done that day. With time, the foot's throbbing subsided and I had such fond memories of a fun race. A change of pace can do that, you know.

No Knee Surgery, But Not Running

An article I recently read, "Running, Knee Surgery, and Life," was so timely and true to me. Except for not having knee surgery, the same miserable down time from running was also my fate. During a 5K race in mid-June I injured myself with a strained gluteus muscle that shut me down from running. This injury later evolved to include the hamstring. Result? A double dose of mega pain and no running.

Therefore, I tried walking just to fool myself into thinking that I could still move forward as a road warrior. Who was I kidding? It just plain hurt too much to run. Little by little, I tried adding segments of running, like 0.1 miles, 0.2 miles, and so on, while walking most of the time. For one who likes to travel in the fast lane, walking my route took forever and a day. I couldn't race and my cheerful demeanor gave way to being personality minus. Yes, it's amazing how running defines our life and who we are.

By September I could run most of my 3.5 mile route, albeit painful and painfully slow. I began to feel like a runner again. My gait was awkward but being doped up on painkillers was not a daily option. The big question loomed: Could I even consider running the hilly Adirondack Marathon on the 21st, an event I had registered for and planned for months earlier? I know many of you could already hear the loose screws rattling in my head. Relying on Aleve and an ibuprofen supplement, I gave it my all and finished a very slow 6:06:30. I just had to see if I could do it cold turkey. Battling fatigue and not having long distance mileage on my legs did not make the trek easy. I guess loose screws rattled loud and clear that day!

A mere three weeks later I had to decide whether or not to run a long-planned half marathon in Murfreesboro, Tennessee with my youngest son. A no brainer! Without adequate training, I would again challenge myself. Although fatigue was an ongoing problem, pain was pretty well controlled during the 2:36:38 time it took me to finish, placing second 70-74. Time-wise, I kept a patient Roy waiting and worrying again. That man is definitely a candidate for sainthood!

Slowly my labored breathing has settled down and going forward with my feet is becoming more natural. I couldn't believe how rapidly downhill my running fitness went these past few months. It was a rude awakening to have to struggle so much to do something that once came so naturally. I felt like I was running with a ball and chain on my ankles. My long stride was non-existent and I struggled just to run a short distance. Nothing clicked. I recall these words of Marilyn Vos Savant: "Being defeated is often only a temporary condition. Giving up is what makes it permanent."

I have been undergoing ultrasound therapy, which healed the injured area and is slowly helping the sore hamstring. I try to be ever so faithful in doing my stretching exercises by telling myself, "You gotta do what you gotta do." Without medication I hurt but I do smile more. The open roads still beckon. I am so much like my dad was - never stubborn, just persistent.

My aged bones and body seem to ache more when I awaken each morning. The zip, zest, and zeal of better years seem more subdued. Trying to make the best out of a negative situation is far better than being idle and feeling sorry for myself. An unknown author penned these words: "Courage isn't always a lion's roar. It is sometimes the heart at the end of the day saying . . . I will try again tomorrow."

The road not taken calls.

A Sidestep Here or There

It happened one fateful day, on January 27, 2010, a cold winter weekday with strong, buffeting winds. It was much too cold to stop running to check a problem with my shoe and foot position and leg achiness. The more I ran, the more the leg pain intensified. I could barely walk the last two miles home and limped with each painful footstrike. End result was a calf and hamstring injury with some knee involvement. This is the plague of runners everywhere who believe that they can do any distance and outrun any pain.

The first round of physical therapy sessions eased the pain. Of course, I quickly formulated plans to resume running. No such luck. You see, Roy and I decided to do a four to five mile walk during the morning of the big snowstorm on February 25th. Our mission: try to find a copy of the day's newspaper. Can't miss the informative weekly column on running. With my sore right leg still mending, I tried to navigate a large snow mound, only to awkwardly lose my balance and feel a sharp pain in my knee. My sore leg just got worse. Now a sprained/pulled ligament was the suspected culprit. Physical therapy sessions were extended and I felt miserably grounded. By this time, my sanity was being tested to the nth degree. Roy remained ever so patient as my bubbly personality plummeted.

Walking didn't "cut it" for me, so in early April I tried running a couple of shorter distances, followed by two longer runs. A 15K race loomed on the horizon and this was my racing goal. I should have heeded a running friend's famous words of wisdom: "Runners are dumb and the longer they run the dumber they become." While up to four miles was doable, but not pain free, doing the two longer runs was my Waterloo. Again! A subsequent visit to my orthopedist meant knee X-rays and an MRI, the latter being so loud that I thought I was in a war zone. These tests indicated no fractures, some ligament involvement, a small meniscus tear, and arthritis, the scourge of many senior runners.

Running has always been my relief valve from stress. Running connects me with Mother Nature and the creatures that abound. I've learned to "talk" to crows, squirrels, and those big, ugly klutzenflappers. I've watched crows relentlessly and noisily chase our resident hawk. I've learned to enjoy the high-pitched voice of the cardinal and the raucous noise of the blue jay. Being out of commission meant that I could not enjoy these simple pleasures. During my walks through town and the village I've had people ask, "You're not running anymore, Erika?" or "Why haven't I seen you running like I used to?" or "How come you're not running today?" It looks like I'm on everyone's radar these days. Three months is a long time to be away from the running scene.

I've tried running a bit but it is hard to limit my enthusiasm. Roy and I lament our turtle pace. The long road back is ever evolving, as are we. Let's hope one day we can pound the pavement with gusto. Still, the road not traveled beckons and we must answer the call.

Downsizing My Running

I knew it would be sooner or later, but I hoped for later rather than sooner. I am referring to having to cut back on my running distances. It concerns my orthopedist's orders not to run anymore versus my decision to "keep on truckin'" on the open roads. While I knew my sore knee would get worse and the discomfort and pain more prevalent, the runner in me wanted to keep this lifestyle alive. Therefore, I made a compromise. To continue running, I would promise myself that my stride would be shorter (easy to do as I can't fully extend or straighten out the affected leg) and my pace would be slow. Pushing off on the bad leg helped me succeed in the former. However, going slower was a hard mental and physical adjustment.

It was a bold decision and a scary one when I decided to run my first race in 2011, the Winter Run five miler in February, followed by the Ed Erichson five miler in March. I know. I overstretched my boundaries with my boundless enthusiasm. The runner in me kept whispering, "Go for it." So I did.

As 2011 progressed, I allowed myself to continue to run with a lot of trepidation, yet smiling broadly with each forward footstrike. I could tolerate the ever present knee discomfort as long as the runner in me could continue to run. Well, let's call my turtle pace "quasi-running" even though I am so humbled and blessed to still achieve winning age group awards.

Preserving the affected knee was necessary so I concentrated on running shorter 5K distances, each race being a gamble. Much slower finishing times were hard for my psyche to initially grasp. However, I have since accepted this situation as long as I can continue to be a runner. A recent quote from Pat Summit, the University of Tennessee's winningest women's basketball coach and recently diagnosed with Alzheimer's disease, gave me the additional encouragement I needed. She said, "It is what it is, but it will be what you make it." Now, downsizing my running is okay. Really okay.

Chapter Six - Variations on the Theme

"For life to be meaningful you must have a challenge." – Author Unknown

Running News Flash! Roy Beats Erika!

It had to happen sometime. With his long legs, stride, and good short distance speed the inevitable occurred. Roy beat Erika in the Main Street Mile on a sweltering and humid afternoon on July 4th. Where did he get his speed? His energy? Was it because he recently turned 65? Was it that AGELESS WONDER inscribed ribbon that he got for his birthday? Was it that nutrient Power Bar? Was it the dripping beads of perspiration that fell to the pavement in puddles as he whizzed by, slowing those behind him? Or was he being chased by Mad Dogs and Englishmen? Whatever the reason, the results will forever stand to show that Roy beat Erika on her own local turf. With her previous times of 7:16, 7:07, and 7:15 to his 7:42, 7:49, and 7:49 the Goddess of Running could not outpace Roy this year. His fabulous PR of 7:18 was two big ticks faster than her slower 7:20. This leaves Erika to wonder what will his fleet feet do next? All you guys in the 60-69 age group have been put on alert. Ageless Wonder Abraham is on a roll. Are you listening, guys?

Track Trekking – The Onteora Mile

The words "Come and see what your little legs can do" were printed on the race application for the 2001 Onteora Mile. It was an invitation and a challenge to all runners.

The race director put so much energy into this race with the desire to "go the extra mile," which certainly turned this one short mile race into a big, classy event. The camaraderie among the runners was evident as we all cheered for each other. What may look easy really takes a lot of stamina.

There were five heats for the adults. The pressure to run under 5:30 was thrilling to watch as the fastest runners did this first heat. I opted for the last heat because it's the most relaxed one and we were jokingly dubbed "the caboose runners." My time was 7:26 (first 60 plus). My reward: a bottle of wine.

It's so much harder to run a mile on the track than to run a race on pavement. This event tests one's leg speed and is such a fun event.

"Come see what your little legs can do" in the future.

A Tribute to "Wonder Girl"

When I initially started running and racing my youngest son gave me the nickname of "Weed" and a co-worker dubbed me "Wonder Weed." It is the name that was imprinted on my T-shirt when I ran my first New York City Marathon in 1987. Memories of this all came back to me at a 5K race. When I saw the running progress made by a woman runner I immediately dubbed her "Wonder Girl." Her husband concurred, and that's why I'm writing this.

I think I first noticed her at a 4K race in 1997. She certainly looked younger than I did, so I didn't have to worry about our age group competition! Since then I have seen her run in many races. While her husband is blessed with fleet feet, she doggedly completed each race and always managed to smile. Her nature was quiet and unassuming, and it was obvious that she liked to run. This impressed me.

Over the last couple of years her times have slowly dipped. Yet I sensed that completion of a race and being in an event alongside her husband were more important than her actual finishing times.

At this race I happened to be near the finish line when she came in. I said aloud, "Wonder Girl." Her husband proudly gave me her time of 30:22. She came very close to breaking 30 minutes on a very hilly course. It just struck me that she really earned the title of "Wonder Girl."

The running community can embrace her for the sheer joy she brings to the sport. While supportive of her husband's running, she shows us in her own quiet way why we run. It's not just the time, it's the moment of doing it.

The Sweatheart Challenge Race

The race director's running feats do the talking for him. For his race in mid-February, it was the sound of 50 pairs of running feet that resonated in unison at this inaugural three mile "Sweatheart Challenge" event. Their presence and participation spoke volumes of this first annual run and its future evolvement.

It was brisk and cold, barely in the upper teens at the start of the race. As was aptly noted on his race application: "Yup, it's cold, but what better way to celebrate Valentine's weekend than running a race with your sweetie in the freezing cold, complete with icy winds off the nearby creek? Hey, at least it's not a 25K . . . it's not even 5K!!" Fortunately, pre-race warm-ups could be held in a nearby building, site of race day registration and gathering of runners. The T-shirts were devoid of advertising, making the cupid with bow and arrow and the surrounding red hearts logo the focal point of attention. Very clever, I thought.

Old and young alike lined up at the start. It was refreshing to see so many younger generation runners wearing their high school's sweatshirts there. It was also gratifying to see more mature and talented runners blending comfortably in with the young crowd. Since my three adult sons claim I'm eternally 21, I guess I don't fit in with this "older" category. However, at the youthful age of 68, I was the oldest female, which suited me just fine. I'll always be a kid at heart and running reinforces this for me.

I was impressed with the speed of the leaders, envying their pace as they were on the return portion and I hadn't even gotten to the midpoint turnaround! One girl went out like a shot from a cannon and I couldn't keep up with the lightning speed of either her or several others, all of whom I quickly lost sight of.

Medals were awarded to the age group winners and I was thrilled to win (60-69) in 27:21. I was not the fastest that day but happy to be a finisher.

Hometown USA 5K Race

There's something about a small town or local race that warms the heart. Perhaps it's the proximity to one's home or the friendly atmosphere or the flat, fast course that winds through the village and passes near a gate at West Point. Maybe it's the low key nature of the event or the race staff and volunteers who make all participants feel special. Perhaps it's the patriotism in one's heart and the red, white and blue decorations that abound.

The Hometown USA 5K race, which is held annually around the Fourth of July weekend and is part of the town's Independence Day celebration, is such an event. While there are a number of races occurring during this particular patriotic weekend, I always choose to run this event.

If it is hot, participants can get cooled off with a hose spray at the midpoint. A few spritzes of cold water can go a long way to rejuvenate sluggish legs and give one the impetus to keep moving. The roads are devoid of most of the main traffic flow and runners are safe to move at their own speed.

It's not an elaborate event, but one which heralds the patriotic nature of the weekend. Winners in all age groups get their award medals with red, white and blue ribbons draped around their neck and are given a warm congratulatory handshake. A real nice homey touch.

Many people congratulated me for my new age group award and expressed surprise that I was 60. Hey, I'll take all the flattery I can get at this age! I was second woman overall this year, beaten by a very gracious 39 year old runner from Pennsylvania. Her family is from the area and she remembered me from previous years. She congratulated ME and said I was her inspiration. She passed me with less than a mile to go.

Also, after I went through the finish line chutes, I asked a young lad of about nine years of age to please untie my shoelaces for me. Bending down was not what my body wanted to do at the moment.

These are some examples of the personal touch at this race that made me proud to be a participant.

The 2002 5K Winter Series Summary

Race #1: There were no signs of earlier predicted nasty weather conditions.

As I approached the campus area the wind seemed to have whipped up right before my eyes. A warm-up run had me buffeted against the cold winds. The starting area had all participants lined up at the base of the little trestle bridge while the wind blasted us head-on.

Yes, this was the wind we had to run into! Many times during the race the wind pushed me back, negating my ability to move my feet in a fast forward direction. I thought about the song "Blowin' in the Wind." Someone once told me to pump my arms and the legs would move faster. Not this time. The one thing moving faster than my legs was the finish line clock as it ticked the minutes. My time: 26:05.

Race #2: It was clear, sunny and unseasonably warm and balmy for this late January day. So many runners wore shorts, a testimony to the sun's warmth. While there were still windy areas on the course, they were not a hindrance to moving forward and up all the hills. A volunteer was positioned at the bottom of the last hill giving verbal encouragement. Good to see Zen Master again at the finish line, full of enthusiasm as each runner came in. I may not be a running speedster anymore but I still harbor the same respect for this hilly course. My time: 25:03

Race #3: Runners go for it in all kinds of weather and the conditions were probably favorable for everyone. Although dreary and overcast (who needs to have sun shining in their eyes?), temperatures were around 40 degrees and the windy areas were quite bearable. Without speed I am still enjoying reaching the finish line. The welcome home cheers have been very uplifting.

For this Valentine's race there were special heart-shaped cookies with pink frosting and white icing words like I LOVE TO RUN, NICE LEGS, I LOVE YOU etc. I chuckled as I read them all . . . and ate two! Someone's heart was really in the right place. Photos of runners from this race were available as freebies. My time: 25:29.

Race #4: Another perfect day for running. Temperatures were again in the 40s, wind was minimal, and shorts were the attire for the more adventurous participants. This was also the awards day for age group winners. My time: 25:19 (first 60-69).

I am grateful to all who did so much that I could run these races which are part of my journey as a woman runner.

Ramblings from the Back of the Pack (a.k.a. The Challenging Summer Cross Country Series)

I really don't enjoy running on trails. The potential for twisted ankles, broken bones, insect bites, poison ivy, and other trail obstacles are not my cup of tea. However, I decided to run the trail series as emotional healing therapy. Here's how the races went:

Race #1

It was held on the Rail Trail in Ulster County. I arrived early, feeling very apprehensive of the unknown. Of course, there were no portable toilets. How dumb of me to ask! Instead, I was advised to find the best bushes. There were so many runners. I couldn't believe there were that many crazies like myself. At least I was in good company. The race was said to be "about three miles." I learned too late not to believe what the race director says. The roots, mud, water, and rocky uphills made me repeat aloud, "I don't believe it." I followed a runner with a bright yellow shirt and even managed to sprint to the finish - sort of.

Race #2

Another trail run surprise. This misery in reverse was "about four miles" of surviving the previous route in the opposite direction with a bit more added. It was very dusty on the back trails and my throat was irritably scratchy. I played hopscotch with the exposed roots and rocks on the narrow trails. Forget about running at speed. This was another test of survival for my legs. This run led me to believe that I definitely am not bio-mechanically agile enough for this nonsense.

My aching quads reminded me of the punishment they endured.

Race #3

The trails at Williams Lake offered more surprises. Early on, my nasal passages got a strong whiff of damp mold, moss and rotten tree bark and limbs. This run had so many uphills after the Bat Cave, so named for its bat inhabitants. Not by any stretch of the imagination was I a graceful ballerina on the hills and very narrow trails. My arms flailed in uncoordinated directions while my feet longed for firmer terra firma. Another confirmation that trails and I do not mesh well. I am still finishing at the back of the pack, but I AM finishing. Four days later my calves and quads were still sore.

Race #4

At last week's race I mentioned to a runner how blessed we had been with such great weather, to which he replied, "It rarely rains for these races." Well, this day Mother Nature unleashed a torrent. I thought about a 60K race I once ran in Central Park in the pouring rain. After 6 hours and 22 minutes of being soaked I looked like a shriveled prune. I do not like to look like a shriveled prune. At 62, age will do this on its own so I don't need any more help from Mother Nature, thank you. Another run, in reverse but longer and very muddy and slippery. Again the Bat Cave was dark and foreboding. With each miserable footstrike I prayed for solid ground and often grabbed low-hanging branches and small trees for support. I finished with a sloshy sprint and at the back of the pack. Everyone wore a nice coat of pure, unadulterated mud. I don't know who is crazier - the runners who participate in these events or the originator of this madness.

Race #5

Before the race started, I spoke about having a twin sister, prompting comments that perhaps she and I both have been running portions of the trails. Hey! One never knows! A heavy dose of humidity and overcast sides added to the challenge of a longer run. The Summit Trail again. I did not look up for bats but rather looked down for places to plant my feet in the still slippery Bat Cave. There was a small section on the trail where there was some very cold air. I was tempted to stop and cool off a bit. I was still content to stay in the back of the pack. A young runner who just squeaked by me said I inspired her, which made me feel good. Anyhow, it was said that Race #6 was to be held off the trails and on paved roads and about six miles. Until then the runners will remember being covered in beads of sweat after Race #5.

Race #6

The weather had all the negativeness it could hold, being that it was unbearably hazy, HOT, and humid. What a relief it was to run on level ground! Since this was really a fun run times were not important. For once I said, "The heck with racing; I'm going to go at a snail's pace for a change and enjoy every minute of it." And yes, I really could smile. Thanks to all for the healing therapy of trail-running craziness.

The Race With a Hill

It all sounded so innocent when I checked the upcoming race calendar - a race with a hill. The distance of 4.4 miles and the location fit the bill. Why not give it a try? I need shorter races to help prepare my breathing and running legs for tackling the longer distances. This seemed ideal.

When the race application came I put it aside for future use. It was hung where I could easily see it so as to not miss it. Isn't it amazing how organized runners can be? As a side note, I did not put the income tax forms where they could easily be seen. That tells you where my priorities lie!

Having previously done the Viking 10K race there, I knew that the area was a runner's paradise, with some hills, no traffic problems to worry about, and plenty of beautiful scenery. I liked the country setting. With all this in mind, I preregistered with eager anticipation. It was only as I read further that I saw the course description: "A 4.4 mile loop through scenic towns. Rolling hills, including one which challenges the lungs." If the hill would challenge my lungs, then I, in turn, would challenge the hill. You see, I am determined to test my breathing to the nth degree because a number of my races were "Did Not Finishes" (DNFs) due to the "I just can't breathe" response. With this problem in the past I concluded that I need to make my lungs work harder and better. Since eliminating all immunotherapy, inhalers, etc. and substituting extra hydration measures, I've been able to race comfortably again, albeit a bit slower. My motto: "Hills, here I come!"

Shortly before race day a friend and I were discussing our upcoming race plans. I casually mentioned that the 4.4 Miler was on my agenda. He then not so casually mentioned THE HILL. "You're doing THAT race? It has a real bad hill." He must have read my mind because he described the hill this way: "On a scale of one to ten it's an eight or a nine." An eight or a nine? What am I getting myself into?

On race day the weather cooperated perfectly with nice coolish temps and no wind problems. I lined up at the start with the rest of the participants. One runner warned me to be prepared for the big, bad hill at about a mile or so into the course. He also mentioned that just when you think you've reached the top, it veered sharply to the right and continued upward again. It was too late for second thoughts now. I was committed to run THE HILL.

The course is interesting. The first mile is scenic going along a level road which parallels the river for a while. So pretty and peaceful that you want to relax and enjoy it all. But not for long. It's a gradual approach that lets your legs know when the incline starts. Then it just goes up and up and up.

The good news is that the upward portion does end, with the rest of the course being mostly level with a few more ups and downs. If what goes up must go down, the the last part of the race is well worth it. It's a nice downhill portion, then a short trail run up to the finish line area.

I recall yelling out "I'm coming, I'm coming" as I approached the finish line. It felt so good to be cheered on by all the volunteers. It was equally nice to say "I did it."

This is a casual low-key type race that brings you back to all the reasons why you run. Because it really is fun. A race doesn't have to be large or glitzy to be successful. It's the feelings one gets afterwards that count.

I had real good feelings.

A Day at the Summertime Poughkeepsie Races

If the Running Gourmet shows up you can bet there's probably food after the race. Well, he was there and there was food. These races, a two miler and a 10K, both with a challenging hill at the start, offer something for everyone. It's just a great way for runners and their families to get together, eat a bit (or a lot!) and share camaraderie.

After a brief hiatus the race director brought these races back on the 2001 running calendar. Therefore, in mid-June, my mission was to run to finish the 10K, not to race against the clock. You see, the 10K race has been my nemesis as it has inevitably frustrated me. It was the agony of defeat. Three strikes and I was out.

Although I successfully ran the 20K event in 1994, I couldn't finish the 10K race for the next three years. In '95 and '96 I had to drop out after about two miles and reached about four miles in '97 only to succumb to heat exhaustion. An air-conditioned ambulance transported me to the finish line area. This was the ultimate defeat. Tears flowed like Niagara Falls.

While the earlier demons still haunted me I was glad to have a chance at redemption this year. I had to conquer the fears of the past. I had to overcome the heat and humidity ever present for these June races. It was good to see so many familiar faces. Even though the humidity was wickedly high and the temperature too warm, seeing them all made me feel good. Fellow runners can do that for you. It was wonderful to have a nice long downhill shortly before the finish. A friend who ran the two miler was there with his trusty camera. I had to smile when he said, "Gotcha Erika!"

As for me? It sure felt good to reach the finish line on my own two feet!

Chapter Seven - Soaring with the Turkeys

"Our aspirations are our possibilities." - Robert Browning

Why I Chose to Focus on This Race

I developed a love affair of running with the turkeys, doing 18 straight years (1992 through 2009) of this annual arduous trek aptly called the Turkey Trot. It quickly became my "must do" race every Thanksgiving Day. That is why I have written these articles on my trials and tribulations of the 25K race, as well as my battles with the whims of Mother Nature and the unforgiving hills. Many times, while approaching the hills with no end in sight, I felt like I was looking straight up to heaven. There were many silent prayers and utterances of "Why am I doing this?" My rebelling knees and tortured quads were not as silent in their zone of agony. Runners have to do what is in their heart and I was grateful to celebrate a day of thanks by reaching the finish line with the grin of the Cheshire Cat at these races.

Mother and Son Run the Turkey Trot 25K

You can tell when the "turkeys" have arrived by the usual commotion at the Turkey Trot races every Thanksgiving Day morning. It's the time for the annual migration to keep a holiday tradition alive. Thus it's not unusual to see participants from near and far ready to converge at the start to strut their stuff.

After running the 25K since 1992, we concluded that the hilly race is not a trot (where one hurries, runs) but rather a trek (where one travels slowly and laboriously). It's the hills that define the course which in turn defines one's speed. The weather, which is usually at its worst for the race, didn't disappoint us - it was damp, rainy, cold, and miserable again.

This year my youngest son, Greg, left his comfortable abode in peaceful Tennessee to do this ultimate running challenge. He was duly forewarned. Greg donned gray cotton shorts while I preferred the warmth of black lycra tights. We shared the same determination to reach the finish line and unceremoniously gritted our teeth as we waited in the cold for the start. YES, there were doubts . . .

We ran side by side matching stride for stride until the first hill at one and a half miles where Greg decided to leave me and give it a kick up the long hill. He took off like a bolting stallion while I plodded along until we met again. At mile five Greg's youthful energy outmatched my aging footstrikes and he led the way. From then on I shadowed those gray shorts. I openly chuckled when Greg raised both arms in jubilation at the eight mile mark. (He later said there was no half way mile mark, so he celebrated at eight). The onslaught of more hills came and I still managed to keep those moving gray shorts in sight, albeit from a distance.

Eventually the gap between us shrunk and at the 12 mile mark I edged ahead. His words of "my butt hurts" were met with my words of "I'm losing it too and my leg and hip hurt." We shared our pain and woe and damned all the hills while still trying to keep that competitive spirit alive.

The gap between us slowly widened and I was serenely alone in my thoughts counting the few miles left and relishing the downhill portion. I saw no one ahead of me and dared not turn around lest those gray shorts zipped past me without a warning. If running is in our genes, so is tenacity. Still, a mother's concern never left me. So, when I approached the high school and saw Roy, all I could say was, "Go look for Greg, he's out there somewhere."

Finally the gray shorts appeared in the parking lot and I ran to yell encouragement. The determination in his stride was evident. He reached the finish line. It was Greg's longest run ever. Bear hugs were in order. Roy used his camera to capture a special moment between mother and son.

On the Long Road with the Turkeys

I don't know why it is. Perhaps I'm just another crazy runner who thinks she belongs among the turkeys on Thanksgiving Day. Somehow it's become a special occasion for me to run this 25K race and this year was my tenth consecutive 15.5 mile challenge.

When I started my Thanksgiving Day tradition, a long time race director was in charge. Several years ago a new race director took over the helm, keeping the race tradition, as well as my own, alive and well. The Turkey Trot races seem to continue to be popular and he has a fine command of the intricacies and work involved in his role as race director.

This year the weather blessed and surprised the runners. It was neither the usual chilly, damp, and rainy variety, nor the bitter cold and windy kind, both so common at this time of the year.

My youngest son, Greg, came up again from Tennessee to make it another challenge of the hills between us. The race to the finish was reversed two years ago when I got there first. This time Greg took off like a charged rocket aimed at the top of the hill at the first mile. He was flying. After the fourth mile I never caught a fleeting glimpse of him again. Of course, this 34-year-old speedster outran his mother by more than 11 minutes and earned this year's bragging rights.

The hill at the twelfth mile has become a real killer hill while the others before it are a prelude that lets my body know that it's already 63 years old. Never again will I see a PR of 2:01:46 or place second or third overall among the women. The turkey trot is now a much slower turkey trek, that's for sure. Greg hopes to challenge me at two-year intervals. Let the turkeys prevail!

The Turkey Trot Races - A Thanksgiving Day Tradition

It's always a challenge to face Mother Nature and the tortuous hills, especially on the 25K course. The whims of Mother Nature do not usually work in favor of the runners. On Thanksgiving morning it's generally either very cold and windy or rainy, damp, and cold. Therefore, we must give thanks to the race director and all the selfless volunteers who brave this day's uncertain elements so that runners like myself can participate.

Since this was my eleventh consecutive year of tackling the rigorous 25K course, I decided to go back in time and see how I described the weather for these past years. This is what I recorded as taken from my logbooks:

1992: Rain, heavy at the 9-10 mile hill area, but moderate rain all the way.
1993: Very cold; strong headwinds made all uphills very hard.
1994: Cold, about 35°F, took legs a good mile or more to warm up.
1995: Cold but bearable.
1996: Cold, about 20°F, and mostly windless.
1997: Very, very windy. Almost the whole way it was strong headwinds.
1998: Rain, muggy and warm for the first several miles, but heavier rain and colder the rest of the way.
1999: Cool, about 50°F, rainy (especially at the start) and a bit windy.
2000: Cold and windy, less than 30°F.

2001: Cool, sunny, 40s, nice running weather. Note: this was an anomaly for sure.

2002: Sunny but very cold, about 14°F; winds (headwinds) picked up on hilly back roads at about 10 miles.

That runners continue to support these races is testimony to the spirit and resiliency of the athletes and a tribute to all those volunteers who work to keep these races on the calendar. This year much-needed commemorative gloves were given to the participants.

In conclusion, I must admit that some years I've felt like a trotting turkey strutting its feathers. Other years it's more like the cooked bird in a pan variety. The unpredictable whims of Mother Nature can do that to you, you know. Running these races on Turkey Day gives one a good reason to indulge without guilt afterwards.

The Day the Turkeys Trotted

A cold, crisp air was present for the 28th Annual Turkey Trot races. These races serve one special purpose on Thanksgiving. They allow runners to run first and indulge themselves later, thereby erasing all feelings of gluttonous guilt. Sort of a placating way of making us feel good about over-indulging in the bountiful harvest of food and drink. It is then that we feel like stuffed turkeys.

This year's event was akin to previous ones. Early in the week the temperatures were warm and mild. Yet, as seems to be the pattern, the weather suddenly turned cold as if Mother Nature dared us to ignore this sharp drop in temperature. Be prepared for hats, gloves, and layers of clothing in a multitude of colors. For the spectators these colors become only a blur as the faster runners zip ahead of other slower runners. For us back-of-the-packers we provide onlookers and fellow runners with a longer look at the palette of colors we wear.

We take to the roads to become the trotting turkeys, colorful in our own attire, yet seeking another runner's brightly colored hat or shirt or jacket to follow. With the beauty of autumn long gone it is these bright colors ahead that define the course, how it ambles around bends and winds up and down over many hilly sections. Just when we think we may have taken a wrong turn a runner up ahead appears, reaffirming our decision to follow THAT road when there are no visible directional arrows. We feel strangely safe in following that particular blur of color running ahead of us.

The first time I ran the 25K course, it was easy to follow the bright orange T-shirt worn by a male runner that kept me focused on the correct route. I can still recall that moment of panic when I lost sight of him just as the road veered to the left. Not only did I not know where I was, I did not know where I was going either! More panic for this turkey. Not to worry however. A few seconds later the moving blur of orange reappeared. Whew! Did I breathe a sigh of relief.

This year there was an equal array of colors to lead the way and I eagerly sought them out. However, with quicker footstrikes than mine, each object of color soon left me behind. I focused on a runner wearing a pastel colored tie-dyed singlet as an outer garment. It was easy to spot him because we were never too far apart. At about the midway point another runner wearing a bright pink T-shirt and red cap passed me. After a short time he, too, left me behind.

The miles crept up. I felt all alone on many parts of the course as bends and hills separated me from those runners ahead of the pack. There were four of them and I missed not seeing them. They had all given me something visible to focus on. Then at the base of a long unforgiving and fortitude-testing hill just after the 12 mile mark I caught a quick glimpse of all four of my leaders. We all seemed to be tackling this last significant hill without too much gusto. Our zip was zapped a long time ago. At least mine was!

I overcame the temptation to power-walk and even managed to keep the quartet of runners in sight for quite a while thereafter. Eventually, however, they too were history.

I think it's the challenge of the 25K course that fascinates me. Hence, I return year after year to once again become a trotting turkey. It must be that unsettled runner in me that thinks only turkeys are around on Thanksgiving.

On second thought, perhaps that's what it's really all about . . . trotting with the turkeys.

Turkey Trot Thanksgiving Day Races

Running the arduous 25K race has been a Thanksgiving Day ritual for me for a long time. I'm sure there are a good number of other runners who have done likewise. The event can humorously be called the annual trek of the turkeys.

The course starts and ends in Freedom Plains. I think I fell in love with this very hilly, quad-aching course the first time I ran it. It certainly can boast of having a peaceful countryside setting as well as unforgettable challenging hills. The only variable has been Mother Nature's whims in dealing us cold, windy temperatures or cold, damp rainy weather. Either way one must battle Mother Nature as well as the late mileage killer hills. They make the earlier inclines a snap.

This year it was cold, brisk, and windy. Good breathing air for the runners but not comfortable temperatures for the many wonderful volunteers. Without their help and presence, turkeys like myself could not do this trot.

I have seen my times flip-flop from highs of 2:01:46 in 1993 and 2:05:21 in 1994 to lows of 2:28:26 in 1998 and 2:29:19 this year. Last year's race was special because my youngest son trekked up from warm Tennessee to challenge his ever-lovin' mother in the 25K. I can still hear him swearing at the hills! He was forewarned. It was a real turkey chase scenario with Greg a few minutes behind me at the finish. Old turkeys never die, they just trot on and on.

On several occasions Roy has run the five mile race which has its own miserable hills on the course. We both owe a debt of gratitude to all the volunteers who work the races so we can run.

I can't envision Thanksgiving Day without these races, especially the challenging 25K. It certainly justifies having a feast later in the day.

Another Year at the Turkey Trot Races

It was a day blessed with nearly ideal running conditions, the best weather that I can remember for the Turkey Trot since I started running the 25K, with clear blue skies, brisk fresh air, and temperatures in the mid-30s. I bathed in the warmth of a sunny sky at the start. It was wonderful to have a race day devoid of wind, bitter cold temperatures or rain. I counted my blessings, as did the other runners.

I also counted the miles, the hills, the money I found (22 cents) on the course, and the time it took me to conquer that last uphill at about mile 12. It was a long time trekking upward. I counted a number of Black Angus cows in a pasture on a back road. I had fun making mooing sounds at them and then chuckled at their twitching ears while wondering if they were actually listening. Hey, if I can imitate crows and squirrels and confuse them on my training runs, why not try confusing the cows? Confusing klutzenflapper birds is another story.

A young woman passed me early on and I marveled at her speed. She said she got her second wind. I told her I was still waiting to get my first wind! At the six mile hill she became a blur, one of many runners who left me behind in the dust of their swift feet. Still, it was comforting to see other runners around me whose pace was more in line with mine. A runner steadily urged his friend not to walk on the six mile hill. Don't walk. Keep running. I passed the duo but left no dust behind with my slower pace.

The maroon headbands that were ordered for the participants were worn by many that day. They also matched my maroon fleece top . . . a fashion statement for sure.

I've learned to have fun as I run the many miles and hills. It's probably why I keep coming back year after year. There are others like myself who also return to tackle the hills. A lesson in Thanksgiving and its meaning.

An Upward Turkey Trek

At one time the turkey commanded enough respect to have a ballroom dance named for it – the turkey trot. Perhaps I identify with turkeys because running the Turkey Trot 25K has become an annual Thanksgiving Day morning ritual for me. While my aged legs may not appreciate all the hills, my spirits always seem to soar and I get real hungry afterwards.

Most of the time the Gods of Inclement Weather rear their ugly heads to bring the earlier mentioned cold, wind, rain, dampness, and misery to the runners. This year, for a while at least, it was actually a mild 60ish degrees day and quite humid. Shorts and short sleeves were the norm. A way of welcoming spring in November. Alas, this did not continue.

Due to the large volume of race day registrants, the 25K start was delayed for more than 30 minutes. My legs, which had run a marathon and then a 10K race within the past 12 days, were eager to get the long trek over with. Since this was the Bob Rother Memorial Run, I wanted to give it my all in his memory. Bob was a beloved runner and mentor to many in the Hudson Valley. I knew I would be slow and was content to bring up the rear. No heroics this day. Just honoring someone special.

Merrily trudging along, the miles passed ever so slowly. Along most of the way I kept in sight the colorful T-shirts of two male runners and a young girl with pigtails who were ahead of me. Deep purple, royal blue, and bright yellow in that order. Shortly after passing the 10 mile mark, Mother Nature unleashed her fury. A sudden drenching downpour with buffeting winds greeted me and the other slower runners. It is said that turkeys have been known to drown if they look up while it is raining. I kept my head down. Muddy water cascaded across the roadway, appearing to come from all directions. The temperature began dropping as the winds whipped up around me. I was left soaking wet and cold. Ahead was an ominous dark sky. My legs started to talk back. I ignored their anguished pleas of discomfort.

I had some moments of fear when, as I turned left onto Freedom Plains Road, a speeding car deliberately drove close to me as I hugged the side of the roadway. My safe running zone was not so safe. I raised my fists and yelled, "You fool," but to no avail. This surprised me since the course is usually safe with virtually little or no traffic to contend with. It got my adrenaline going at a time when I really needed it.

By the time I neared the end my stride was reduced to the short, jerky steps that a turkey takes. More like an uncoordinated turkey trot. Seeing several volunteers at the finish line brought a smile to my face. As age creeps up, the hills get tougher, my times get slower, and I wonder, albeit briefly, why I keep coming back. Now that the 25K is the Bob Rother Memorial Run, I have to come back as a way of honoring his memory and all that he meant to the running community.

The Snow, the Turtle, and the Turkey Trot

Expect the unexpected. That would best describe the day of this year's Turkey Trot races. With the finicky whims of Mother Nature, any kind of weather can and will prevail.

This year's event brought more snow and chilly temperatures. It was just another reason for me to run faster to reach the finish line!

A light snow created a serene beauty all its own. But it also brought along the potential for slippery roads. As the race director said, white road course arrows along with white road snow was not a good combination for running on the back roads. With this in mind, he made the safe and sound decision to modify the 25K course. The back roads would be avoided, but there would still be the hills, continuing the traditional challenge of a great leg workout.

The modified 25K course consisted of doing the five mile loop three times with some extra footsteps going to and around the cones in the parking lot. We would enjoy the company of the entourage of five mile runners for a brief time only. I caught a glimpse of Roy on his way out as we met at the pinnacle of the infamous hill on my return trip from the first loop. I was going at a turtle's pace and was content to bring up the rear in the 25K. The course soon became all 25K runners again.

A male runner, having finished the 25K, sped past me and up the hills like a gazelle, encouraging all of us as he left dust rather than snowflakes behind. A woman runner's smile greeted me often, as did her words of encouragement. Even when my tired body felt like quitting, I couldn't find it in my heart to do so. With about two and a half miles to go, I overtook two runners and relinquished my turtle's position.

What a pleasant surprise to receive a goody bag at the finish. Usually most post-race refreshments are gone when the slower 25K runners amble in. I thought this was really special. It's evident that the race director goes all out to make the Turkey Trot Races a real runner's event, as I can attest to.

Anatomy of the Turkey Trot Amid the Rain, Wind, and Cold

Blowing rain greeted Roy and me as we left home for the drive to the site of the yearly Turkey Trot races. It was miserable and cold. We parked behind a Lexus vehicle which had this appropriate license plate staring at us: RUN TUFF. This would have to be our modus operandi if the day's foul weather predictions held true.

The Gods of Good Weather did not work in our favor nor did we bask in the sun's warmth. Temperatures were in the mid-30s, it was damp, cold, windy, and with enough rain to last a lifetime. I was concerned about my sore foot but decided to go for the long haul, hopeful that I would be able to ignore any pain with a lot of positive thoughts. As we exited the parking lot, a friend cheered us on and gave me a hearty high five.

I hadn't even reached the two mile mark when the lead pack of the five mile race's runners whizzed by. Shortly thereafter I saw the first woman charge by. I chuckled because my pace was evidently not too fast. Another runner later sped by, again wishing me well. He is an ardent supporter of all runners.

For me, the rain got heavier at about the four mile mark and I concluded that I'd be a wrinkled prune by the time I reached the finish line. As I trudged up the hill at six miles, I saw a hunter, complete with orange vest and rifle and I wished him well. He reciprocated the good wishes. From about mile seven on I was alone on the roads. Then, shortly after I rejoiced after passing the eight mile mark, a runner came from out of nowhere. He was dressed in a sleeveless tank top and shorts. In no time at all he was history.

I sloshed onward and upward, the miles and hills added up and so did the rainfall. The long hill at mile 12 seemed to be an eternal climb. I was so heavy-laden with my wet anorak that all thoughts of speed dissipated. Actually, I felt blessed by the cold rain's soothing effect on my aching heel and by the cooler weather in general. I repeatedly told myself that I was having fun, like a kid playing in the rain puddles. Well, sort of.

As I neared the 15 mile mark, a truck passed, having picked up the last runner somewhere on the course. I finally saw two runners ahead of me that I thought were a mirage a bit earlier. Roy was standing nearby, visible by the large bright yellow umbrella he was holding and ready to capture another wet "Kodak moment" with his camera. The rain felt like freezing pellets hitting me from all directions. I sloshed through more puddles, picked up a lucky heads-up penny and at 2:52:45 on the clock was enthusiastically cheered on by a most welcoming finish line crew. Last but not least.

A few people were still inside the building including a friend staying until the end as he said he would. I felt badly that my turtle speed kept all there for so long. Perhaps next time I should consider hitching a ride on a charging wild turkey. Those turkeys can certainly trot.

Still Doing the Turkey Trot

I'm usually so far behind I think I'm first. This year an earlier start had me as the leader of the pack for the first seven-plus miles. A rare role of race dominance for me. In rapid succession, three runners passed me and my glory was thus short-lived. As I approached the eight mile mark, the first woman whipped by me like a gazelle moving on the African veldt. She acknowledged me with her ever present welcoming smile while never losing her stride. One by one, more runners passed me as I tackled the quad-aching hills. Somewhere around 10 or 11 miles a male friend ran by with a burst of speed and verbal encouragement. I quickly lost sight of him in the winding hills. One positive thing to remember is that all hills have their downsides.

This year's 25K race was my 17th straight trek on the hilly course, including the modified 15 miler in 2005. From 1992 through 1997, starting at age 54 I had to try to place among the top five females to get an award. Although I placed third (2:07:36) in 1992 and second (2:05:21) in 1994, my best time (2:01:46) in 1993 only earned me a sixth place finish and no award. This was heartbreaking. Between 1998 and 2003 I placed among the now top seven women four out of six times. After that my senior years really caught up with me and I became content to happily "bring up the rear."

As for the whims of Mother Nature, race day has usually been cold, rainy and/or miserable, as earlier summarized. In 1993 it was very cold and strong headwinds made all the hills hard to conquer. In 1997 it was very, very windy again. In 1998 it was rainy, muggy, and warm early on, but heavier rain and colder temperatures for the rest of the way. In 2002 it was about 14 degrees, sunny, very cold, with winds that picked up at about the 10 mile mark hill area. What a change in 2004 with high humidity (93%) and warm temps (about 65 degrees) at the start. The day later brought showers with wind and colder temps and pouring rain at about 10 miles. The year 2006 brought rain, heavy and steady at times, with cold temps of about 35 degrees, and for me in my slower pace, freezing rain pellets far the last half mile or so. The forceful rain cascaded across the roadway. In 2007 it was suddenly quite warm and muggy from the earlier rainfall. I wilted in this "heat wave," preferring colder, crisper temperatures.

It's uncommon to see older, senior women run the 25K, and, with two exceptions, I have been the oldest woman finisher. This year, at 70, I think I can claim that record. Even in my early 50s, I could keep up with the best of the younger runners. As the saying goes, "Many a great tune has been played on an older fiddle."

So, bring on the turkeys. This older fiddle still has many great tunes to play.

Chapter Eight - Shifting Gears and Footstrikes

"Two roads diverged in the wood and I, I took the road less travelled by and that has made all the difference."
– Robert Frost

The Inaugural Wurstboro Mountain 30K

On March 30th 2002, an idea became a reality. The Wurstboro Mountain 30K race was a challenge for 107 runners and a successful event for the race director. It was a tremendous undertaking for sure and, as someone said to me, a race for the "crazies." That all finishers received commemorative medals was a touching gesture and an appropriate way of recognizing all who completed this arduous 18.6 miler.

The course was beautiful and serene especially along the Basha Kill area. The uphills were a challenge and the steep downhills were punishing on the feet and knees yet both traversed such a peaceful rural area. Pain was forgotten for a while. Water stations were plentiful and those manned by volunteers provided so much verbal encouragement to the runners. My downfall came when I grazed "The Wall" at mile 14, bumped into it at mile 15, and hit it head-on at mile 16. By mile 18 my body was in the shutdown mode. My spirit was willing but my flesh was pounded. It was dehydration that did me in this time.

The kindness of so many people was overwhelming. Thanks to a course marshal and another volunteer for walking with me to the finish line where I later saw a cheering group of earlier finishers. It as wonderful and heartwarming to get such great support.

My husband was the last runner to come in yet the finish line crew graciously awaited his arrival. So many others kept me up to date on his whereabouts on the homestretch. As a runner I am grateful for everyone who volunteered all those long hours so that I could be a race finisher.

The Hills, the Miles, and the 30K

When I initially wrote about this race, I mentioned that the "crazies" would be back . . . and they were! Nearly 100 runners completed this most challenging 18.6 mile race on the inclines of Wurtsboro Mountain. The steep downhills were a welcoming reward for all the early uphills. This was followed by many undulating miles of scenic backroads with the final 0.6 mile seemingly the fastest.

Mother Nature provided overcast skies, temperatures in the warm 50s and a drizzle that often became a cooling rainfall. I thought about the song "Raindrops Keep Falling On My Head." For me the rain had a pleasant cooling effect. However, the early uphill grade did not bode well with my legs. Nothing in my body wanted to move upward. The thought of dropping out early on weighed heavily on my mind until at about mile two or so when the race director saw me and greeted me with "my hero!" I thought, "Now I can't drop out and disappoint him." My spirits were buoyed along the way when I saw two race officials drive by. So nice to be personally acknowledged. Over the course route I would again be cheered on by them. The same ones who graciously walked me in to the finish line a year earlier when I hit the wall and couldn't get my legs to move. At that time, from mile 14 on, the course was a blur.

This time I was never really alone as I traversed the course. Some light chatter with other runners ensued as the legs moved forward. We all tried to maintain a steady, albeit slower, pace as the miles added up. While on one of the backroads I recall a sign near a house that said "Journeys End." While smiling, I thought, "Yeah, right . . . I still have a long way to go before my journey ends." I stopped briefly to let a roving photographer take a snapshot. A nice pause.

Anyone eager for a good, long and challenging run would be wise to consider doing this event. Who knows, you might even get to keep me company then.

Run Around Briggs Mountain

It was a typical early spring day with good running weather and plenty of hills to look forward to conquering. This was the sixth annual Race Around Briggs, a 7.2 mile trek up, down, and around the mountain and the countryside terrain of Milan, New York.

For the participants it was a test of one's strength, resolve, and desire to get a real good workout. What stood in the way of an easy run were steep downhills and uphills, especially for the last two miles where the uphills were relentless. Hey, what goes up must come down! Thus the final short distance to the finish line was a nice downhill for sprinting if one's weary legs were up to the task.

Roy and I used the challenging terrain as a good training run for upcoming races. I have to take credit for talking him into doing it. Wrong-Way Abraham lived up to his name when he went a bit beyond the last right turn. The ambulance following him honked its horn so he could correct his mistake. We both felt exhilarated at reaching the finish line. It must be our mixed up genes that let us seek out the not-so-easy and non-flat races. It's more fun taking the roads (and hills!) less travelled.

It seemed to be the fun of getting together for friendly competition that fueled the feet of all the participants who turned out for this race.

The Double Van Run

After running the very hilly 7.2 mile Run Around Briggs, I was surprised to learn that several participants were then running the course in reverse as an extra training run. As I soothed my aching quads I thought to myself that they must be nuts. Then came the date for the Double Van event on the race calendar. It honors the memory of a 9/11 hero, a fallen firefighter.

This event is the Run Around Briggs course doubled. More than 14 miles of leg punishment. Getting older and conveniently forgetting those arduous earlier hill climbs, the idea of running the Double Van appealed to me as another challenge to conquer. With the upcoming Turkey Trot 25K looming on the horizon, the hills of Milan seemed ideal for a long training run. Therefore, I convinced Roy to join me in signing up for double the workout we did last time.

On race day I was really psyched up. While my speed would be compromised by the hills, I nonetheless welcomed a slower pace for this challenging run and for my survival. Although sunny, cold, brisk, and breezy, the weather was perfect. My legs were sluggish and when the hills appeared they did not move as fast as in "The Charge of the Light Brigade." When the ambulance drove up behind me I thought, "I must be last, or I must look like death warmed over." Forget speed on the long hilly stretch on Academy Hill. Riding bikes, two course marshals made me envious of their chosen mode of navigating the course.

It was so nice to receive cheers as I reached the turnaround point to begin the second loop in reverse. Assurances were given that they all would wait for me at the finish line. I reminded them that it would be a long wait. I did not lie.

Running down the long Academy Hill section I was relieved to see that there were several runners, including Roy, trekking uphill to reach the turnaround. Whew! I was not last after all. However, my bubble burst when I later learned that I was indeed the last woman, as the others stopped after the first loop. Perhaps they chose to run only one loop rather than have a team person run the second loop. Roy decided that he would just do the one loop, then wait for me with camera in hand to capture a "Kodak Moment" at the finish.

Onward I plodded, following a young lad who had the speed of a gazelle on the hills while I power-walked. With about three miles to go I gradually eased past him and reached the finish line in 2:23. What a tremendous feeling! Never mind that few did the double loop solo. Never mind that I was almost last. I had met my goal of finishing the entire 14-plus miles.

The Hillside 14

The Double Van Run became the Hillside 14 this year with a new venue equal in needed leg power as was with the earlier race. This year, to not only include the hardcore runners, a 5K was added.

Leave it to the brains behind the agony of the Double Van event to again create a masterpiece of quad-aching hills. The course designer referred to an early steep incline as Agony Hill. However, it was not mentioned that Agony Hill included more than one such incline. There were so many uphills that I lost count.

This new course was a real challenging trek that included traversing a horse trail at 11 miles. Its entry point was not easily distinguished so I went where I thought the bright orange arrow pointed. It was a rude awakening, like "Oh, woe is me" at its best. The "trail" was a never-ending maze of mud, large clumped grass, horse droppings, and turns. I felt like I was shuffling my feet through the infamous Area 51 with aliens hovering above me. It was a balancing act of gigantic proportions to keep my feet upright. I had to laugh aloud at how funny I must have looked. Any resemblance to a runner's gait was non-existent. I saw many horseshoe prints and deer tracks but little evidence that runners before me had navigated the course. Still, if orange arrows appeared, I concluded I must be doing something right. The horses were beautiful but probably confused by the crazy runners going by. I paused to admire them.

Since I seemed alone (14 miles is a long, long trek) and bewildered most of the time after about seven and a half miles, I presumed I was the last runner. A lone runner was somewhere ahead of me in the wild blue yonder and I was already passed by several female runners, most doing only half the distance, each part of a team.

I recalled last year's race where I won a prize for being the last woman in, after completing both hilly loops of the Double Van race. This time, the race director high fived me as I approached the finish line in 2:19:52. I had survived the notorious Hillside 14. To my surprise, I was not last, and the race director promptly stated I would not get that award. I jokingly replied, "Well, you can give me the Oldest Runner award." After all, I am 66. Would you believe that's what I got, in the form of a Frisbee toy? You just have to laugh at times like these.

The Monticello Monster Classic

As a veteran of seven previous Monster 10K races, it's easy to see that I like the event. With its unforgiving hills it has managed to become one of my anticipated challenging races in the summertime.

This year the logo of a monster gobbling a running shoe was quite appropriate for me in an abstract way. My polio-affected legs were once again reluctant to perform. Barely into the 10K race, I had no feeling in my lower legs and the pavement seemed so soft and spongy. No competitive racing for me. Therefore, as on other previous occasions, I stopped by the roadside and waited to join up with Roy. Within a short time he felt weak. Our already slow pace became even slower. A snail's pace would have been faster! Roy likened himself to being slower than a hibernating mud turtle. His British humor came through and we laughed. Our goal was to "bring up the rear," however long it took.

On the positive side it's nice to chat with other runners as they eased ahead of us. While side by side with them we learned about the bygone days of the now defunct Concord Hotel and the manicured flower-trimmed road that once graced its entrance. How sad to see the neglected and uncontrolled weeds at this once majestic property.

Somewhere along the course I saw a sign that I thought said "American Casket Company." We sure felt ready for the Box! Closer inspection revealed that the sign actually said "American Gift Basket Company." Another laugh shared. Roy and I took pleasure in admiring the beautiful blue cornflowers and purple loosestrife, so prevalent along the way. We watched a colorful Monarch butterfly flutter by. A "Kodak moment" without the camera.

Our running was not our best or our fastest this day. Yet we enjoyed the race and its many amenities. What an oversized goody bag. What filling post-race food. What patient water stations volunteers, course marshals and police personnel. Although hot and tired, they all cheered us on.

While I can't predict the condition of my legs during training runs or races, I can always appreciate often overlooked sights, togetherness with Roy, and wonderful camaraderie at races. Tears of defeat are replaced by remembering these words of George Sheehan: "The answer to the big question in running is the answer to the big question in life: do the best with what you've got."

Chapter Nine - Beyond The Ordinary

"All hills have their downsides." - Motto of 1997 Smoky Mountain Marathon

Only One Hill

"Only one hill." That's what they said. How well we were to remember these words that were spoken to us at the start of the 7.6 mile run UP Mount Washington. Our elation at being among the 1,000 lottery-picked entrants slowly turned to words like "we're crazy!" whenever Roy and I discussed our plans for going to New Hampshire for this unique road race. Many times we asked ourselves the question, "Why would anyone want to run UP a mountain?" The usual response of "because it's there" just didn't satisfy us. There had to be another reason why so many runners yearly apply to and hope to be accepted into this race.

Well, the answer lies in doing it! It is a race up a mountain so unpredictable in its atmospheric conditions on the summit and so awesome for anyone to attempt to conquer. Billed as the "run to the clouds," it more than lives up to its expectations. The only thing is that we didn't know what to expect!

On the evening before the race we scouted the fog-shrouded mountain, unable to see its majestic appearance because of a heavy rainstorm. It was a rainstorm that was to be with us into the next day. The mountain certainly was not too friendly in greeting us!

On the day of the race, at the base of our "one hill," we chatted with the driver who would later take us down, all the while keeping our fingers crossed that conditions on the summit would be bearable. One runner, a multiple returnee, told us that the toughest part was mental because you soon know, but don't easily accept, that there won't ever be any downhills, only incline . . . after incline . . . after incline. Another runner warned us that "you'll never see so much of your running shoes again."

Sometime after the first steep mile, Roy and I became separated. I dared not look back for him lest the temptation of seeing a downhill be too overpowering to resist. The dense fog was a blessing in disguise because I couldn't see what steep incline lurked menacingly around each approaching bend. Once past the tree line a muddy dirt road awaited me. Ignorance WAS bliss, believe me! I had no choice but to continue going UP and UP. Somewhere, at about six miles into the upward trek, a strong gust of wind blew my lucky Yankee baseball cap off my head. Retrieving it provided the only downhill running I was to do - about 15 feet. My legs cried out for relief but there just wasn't any. "Onward and upward" seemed to be the prevailing battle cry.

The final mile seemed like an eternity. Will I EVER see the summit? You can imagine my thrill when I was greeted by a crowd of well-wishers at what I thought was the finish line. When I reached this jubilant crowd I was greeted with, "You're almost there, only 100 feet and 20 seconds to go. You can do it." I looked up and stared in disbelief at what awaited me - a nightmare come true. The road made a sharp, steep bend, then went straight up to heaven. I remember muttering to no one in particular, "You gotta be kidding!"

Gamely I aimed my feet in the direction of bright flashbulbs and more voices. Not until I was almost under it could I see the finish line clock. What was muggy, rainy, and 70 degrees at the base turned out to be very windy, bone-chilling cold (about 30 degrees with the wind-chill factor), and so densely foggy that visibility was less than 10 feet at the pinnacle. My long trek up "only one hill" was over. Muddy, dirty, wet, cold, and tired, I had conquered a formidable foe in 1 hour, 55 minutes and 20 seconds.

For those runners who like to be at the pinnacle and seek the challenge of getting there, this race is for you. Getting there is ALL the fun!

Foot Power - An Out and Back 50K Race

The forecast of rain and sleet fizzled out, a blue hue colored the skies as gray threatening clouds drifted away, and Rockland Lake State Park came alive in mid January for the third annual Super Bowl Marathon and 50K race. Not only was it the race director's conceived event, but it was a race that belonged to all who participated: the runners, sponsors, spectators, and volunteers. It was one of those events where the threat of winter prevails, where the runners have a chance to keep in shape without the benefit or guarantee of being caressed by the warm, balmy sun. Where participants can greet the New Year with a race guaranteed to be a challenge, to test one's winter level of fitness and stamina, and to give the county its own unique winter marathon. For those energetic runners who wanted even more, there was also the 50K.

I was one of five female runners who chose to "go all the way with the 50K." Just because it was a flat course didn't make it any easier on my knees and legs. After running at what I considered to be a fairly comfortable 20 miles, a twinge of pain in one knee confirmed that a flat route without hills does not necessarily make an easy course. Pounding the pavement mile after mile was an ever-present necessity and my left knee chose to rebel against the torture that I unabashedly forced upon it, causing me to "walk it out" for the last six or seven miles of my 31.1 mile quest.

It was a race where words of encouragement flowed freely, where a number of spectators and volunteers heartily cheered us on and where dedicated volunteers stayed until the end of a long six-plus hours day. I was heartened by the many male runners, most of their faces unfamiliar, who offered words of encouragement or a "thumbs up" sign along the way. Particularly helpful were the words and acknowledgements from two of them as we so often passed during those endless one mile stretches. Equally helpful were the enthusiastic choruses of "Come on, you can do it," "You're looking good," and "Nice going, keep it up" from such cheering sideliners. From Roy I collected my share of on-the-run bear hugs and quick kisses when our paths crossed somewhere along the long course.

A female runner, running a fiercely strong race, was an inspiration with her ever-present passing smile, truly a runner's example of "poetry in motion." Just watching her run gave me that extra push to keep going. I remember the determination of a runner who commented at about the 16th or 18th mile, "That's all for me," but who also continued on, passing me often as he accomplished his goal and finished the marathon. I recall how strong two male runners ran whenever I saw them and how I not so gracefully plodded onward. A woman came and walked alongside me showing possible ways of lessening and alleviating strain on my now very sore knee.

It was a race that took its toll on my knees, legs, and body, but not on my spirit. Even though it meant walking at the end, I was determined to finish what I had started. Being the very last runner did not dampen my spirits or lessen the thrill as I crossed the finish line at 6:00:57. Boy! Was I glad it was over! I could almost hear my vibrating leg muscles singing a loud "Alleluia."

For many, this race belonged to the runners. The melody came from many feet pounding the pavement at a different cadence, the lyrics came from those endless words of encouragement, the song of victory was in every runner's heart, but it was the race director who put it all together to conduct a beautiful "orchestra for the feet."

The Second Time Around - Reflections on an Ultramarathon

The race director for the Super Bowl Marathon and Rockland Lake 50K Ultramarathon must have a direct line to the God of Heavenly Weather. The weather for this year's race was good for the runners - a brisk, cool day with an abundance of sunshine and a tolerable breeze. In retrospect it is difficult to say just what prompted me to again give the pavement a thorough pounding and test my limits of endurance and discomfort. If my aching legs and feet rebelled at the thought of running 31.1 miles, my spirit took delight in meeting this ultimate challenge for the second time.

My training preparations for both of them were about the same. I continued to run consistently after completing the New York City Marathon in November, adding one additional long run (a 14 miler the first time and a hilly 30K race this time) to my training program. In my mind, running the 50K ultramarathon just seemed like the thing to do at the time.

This year's start consisted of running the additional turnaround distance first, followed by one mile out and back loops. Psychologically I thought this was a good idea. Although I ran strong for the first 13 miles, I soon concluded that I needed to maintain a slower pace for the duration of the remaining distance. Consistency in pace and stride was my plan. Because I turned the sharp corners at the cones with less speed and more care, the previously experienced painful left knee problems did not occur this time. My knees were grateful! Last year my overall feeling seemed stronger and more energetic, but once the knee pain became unbearable, I lost so much time "walking out" the last 6 miles. This year I did not have to resort to any walking.

The repeat out and back course seemed to offer a charm all its own. Overlooking scenic Rockland Lake, it afforded many views to every runner's eyes. This year I enjoyed the pristine beauty of the glistening snow on the roadside (remnants of an earlier snowfall) while the warmth of the sun's rays was a welcomed respite from a fairly strong headwind in the opposite direction. I likened it to the Midas Touch because its warmth soothed and somewhat rejuvenated my tired and aching body. The soles of my feet became sore from repeatedly striking the pavement. Were they still attached to my legs I wondered? I tried not to think about possible blisters forming. As I ran I observed a potpourri of runners, each hoping to savor the thrill of victory. Fellow runners called out words of encouragement, even as they struggled with their own discomforts. We shared a common turf, fought the same battle, and sought a common goal. Mile after mile I ran on. Bit by slow bit the remaining runners dwindled and my miles to go shortened. The end was in sight. With eight miles to go, my body played its own tune of agony as extreme tiredness set in. Whistle a happy tune I did not!

Nearly five hours and twelve minutes after I started, the long run was over for me. It was only after I ceased moving that my legs let me know how much running distance they had endured. My grin became wider than my stride.

I made it! I successfully completed my second ultramarathon, knocking off 49 minutes from my previous time. It was now time to quietly revel in what I had just accomplished . . . and think about getting much-needed rest!

The 25th Annual Whiteface Mountain Uphill Footrace

It's an early June morning in Wilmington, New York. You could see the orange color of the rising sun. Temperatures were in the high 40s already. Still, it could be hot at the base of the mountain and cold on the top. What to wear could be a puzzlement for this 8 AM staring race. We chose not to bring an extra top layer.

Since our motel was a mere 0.1 miles away from the start, Roy and I leisurely walked there. No sense running. We wanted to save our leg power for the long eight mile trek up the Veterans Memorial Highway to the tower on the top. There were 256 registered participants. I briefly exchanged a "hello" with another runner I knew, who then took off like a rocket.

The first three miles to the Tollgate were said to be the steepest – a 10% grade. Our aching legs could attest to this statement. My rocket fuse quickly fizzled. Power-walking with spurts of running became the norm. One can really move forward with swinging arms and long leg strides. It was a more efficient way to move upward.

At mile four the wind picked up and a cold chill engulfed me. Here, the midway point, you could look up and see the roadway and the tower where the finish line was. It seemed to occupy a position that was straight up and the roadway looked so foreboding and so far away. Hey, we made it halfway up already! The chill engulfed me again at the six mile mark.

At several water stops cheering spectators rang loud cowbells or played music to encourage us upward and onward. Once a group of energetic youngsters greeted us with a wave in the middle of the road as we crept by. We traversed several steep hairpin turns as we ascended closer to the top. We had to watch our footing but what magnificent views! I had nice conversations with some equally suffering participants. One woman was doing the race for the 17th time. She was aiming to break two hours so I shadowed her as best as I could (and passed her with a mile to go).

I knew Roy was somewhere behind me but I never looked back. I feared a stop to look downward would be too enticing to turn around and go in that direction. With an aching hamstring, it wouldn't take too much enticing. I managed to pass four others, three who were part of the group I was with and one young guy who just seemed to have run out of steam and was leisurely walking.

The last mile was a mixture of inspiration and determination. One final hairpin stood in the way of getting to the finish. The cheers were loud. I saw the clock and sprinted the final short stretch. I made it in 1:57:57. Approaching 2:20 on the clock, Roy had a burst of energy and reached the finish line in 2:20:23. We both had conquered Whiteface Mountain.

The finish line chutes and clock are dismantled after two and a half hours, so it's a real challenge to get there in time. We made it and were on "cloud nine."

The awards ceremony followed and I was surprised to win my 60-69 age group. The impressive gold medal was attached to a key ring and encased in a black velvet pouch. I felt so blessed.

We are thinking about doing the race again. It certainly is a different kind of pinnacle to reach.

Anatomy of an Ultra - Recover from the Holidays 50K

Between 1989 and 1991 ultra running was in my blood. I ran a 60K in 6:22:41 in the pouring rain and had a PR of 4:53:21 for a 50K. This year when a challenging 50K race again loomed on the horizon, the bug hit me. It was time to go the distance. It would be a test of true grit.

"Oh my, you gotta be kidding," were words I muttered to myself as I attacked the hills of the first loop of the 3.1 mile out-and-back course. Thus, I began running my first ultra in nearly 13 years. Obviously older and slower. Obviously not wiser either. Lord knows why the urge to tackle a 50K race now beckoned me. Perhaps because it was there. Perhaps because it would test my limits. Perhaps because I left some of my brain cells behind. Perhaps because it was January 3rd when in 1988 Roy and I met while running and we celebrate this day by doing an annual run together. A special day!

Race day at Norrie State Park was damp, dark, and dreary, but spirits seemed to be in high gear even when it rained a bit. Some runners opted to start an hour earlier; others, like Roy, opted to complete several loops rather than all ten. For all of us, the race director was a one-man cheering squad. He was later joined by a co-director who, after running the 50K, also stayed until the last runner was clocked in. The race director had promised me that he would wait the six hours or so that I told him it would probably take me to finish. You can't ask for more than that!

I was given a lot of encouragement and moral support on the course and ran strong for the first four loops. My spirits were good even though I had to walk a bit up the first big steep hill on loop #4. I liked the challenge that I had forced on myself and the test of my stamina.

For me some more walking followed on the hills on loop #5. After 15.5 miles my legs were in a shutdown mode and it was an effort to keep on trekkin'.

Power-walking on the hills and some flat areas helped me move forward. However, my spirits remained high even after a runner referred to me as "Mom" (I haven't figured that one out yet). When I thought I could do no more other runners encouraged me to try "one more loop." The co-director's words were also always uplifting and graciously accepted. I don't know how many times he and other runners lapped me.

At the end of loop #6, I felt very chilled and feared for the worst. Roy's cheering as he met me after each loop helped my morale and was a big factor in my decision not to quit. At about loop #7 or #8 I told the runner who called me "Mom" that I could still smile and gave him a big grin to prove it. It came from the heart. Loops #7, #8, and #9 were done at a slow but determined pace interspersed with periods of fast walking. On one of these loops I saw a guy with a dog walking and running ahead of me. I chuckled when the dog's legs suddenly went out from under him on an icy spot. The dog looked so funny but didn't miss a beat. It got right back up. I knew I had to keep doing the same. Just get up and go!

On loop #10, I was able to pick up the pace a bit and walked less, being on an adrenaline high and knowing the end was attainable. My long trek was over when I was clocked in at 6:04:53. WHEW!

As Roy would say, "Jolly good show."

They Don't Have Weather Like This in July

"Simply finishing is the first level of winning. For me, a slow race is better than an incomplete one." I thought these words of Joe Henderson were appropriate to the Recover from the Holidays 50K race.

The day before the scheduled 50K race brought sleet and freezing rain to our area, so I didn't know what conditions to expect on race day morning. It did not take long to see that icy conditions dominated the park's road surfaces. Ice skates were the preferred mode of movement. It was a race director's worst nightmare. My heart sank. How could I ever navigate the hilly course, not once, but ten times? Extreme caution was advised by the race directors on site, one who felt nature's wrath when he made body contact with the ice while setting up course signs. I retreated to the porta-toilet for warmth and to ponder my options, of which returning home was not one of them. A park's department truck appeared and spread sand on some of the icy areas. I still did not know how many other spots would be sanded, but at least we didn't have to glide on the ice in the main parking area. I thought about one race director's earlier dilemma and how he could now proclaim, "Somebody up there likes me." That's for sure!

There were about 30 runners at the starting line ready to battle the cruel whims of Mother Nature. Roy indicated that he hoped to do three loops. I decided to try one loop and "take it from there." Many cautious footstrikes would be needed. It was a challenge to navigate the icy course and hills. At my age, broken bones are not an appealing by-product of a footstep gone wrong. I maneuvered all over the roadway seeking out the least icy spots. The sun made a brief teasing appearance and its warm rays were a godsend. It was music to my ears to hear the race directors say, "There's Erika" as I neared the completion of each loop. This certainly boosted my spirits and, truth be known, gave me the impetus to go on. I likened the race directors to my visible guardian angels.

So many runners offered verbal encouragement along the way and I looked forward to seeing the same faces as we ran in opposite directions. After each loop, Roy would greet me with "Looking good, kiddo" and offer me whatever replenishments I might need. Upon completion of the filth loop, the big question needed answering, so I decided to "go for it." I played mind games with myself. In the parking area the puddles between the ice-coated sides got bigger and deeper. Nowhere to go. It was near the end of loop #6 that my feet got soaked and cold because I could not avoid the lesser of the two evils. Within minutes, I could not feel or move my toes. A cloud cover dominated the sky and it felt so much colder and raw. Gritty pebbles got into my shoes. Ouch. My awkward stance became more tenuous. My nose was running faster than my feet. Survival mode took over.

As I was on loop #8, a guy passed me, saying he was ready to quit at #8 but decided to go for #9 and #10. By this time I was so slow I thought it would be dusk when I finished and I envisioned the park shutting down. A few snowflakes fell and I was chilled to the core. On my last loop, the guy who nearly quit was driving out of the park. He had finished, was grinning from ear to ear, and gave me a thumbs up sign. When

I reached the final turnaround I thought about my mother waving her finger at me from the heavens above while chiding me for being so crazy in my old age for doing this.

I was miserably cold but happy when I finally finished and thankful that the two race directors worked so long and hard to let me savor victory. My time was 6:26:24, which was about the amount of sleep that I got the night before. As for this race, I just wanted to see if I could do it.

You know, they don't have weather like this in July.

A Winter Ultra Race

Feeling apprehensive two days before the 50K race, I decided to reread an article by a sports columnist about his 40 mile race to celebrate his 40th birthday. It was and is a powerful personal account of a determined soul who conquered adversity and nature's cruel elements in his quest to reach a goal.

When race day came, it was a near perfect January day for an ultra. That is until you recall the early morning snowfall that nearly gave the race co-director (and sports columnist) an ulcer. His earlier personal conquest propelled me onward to face the hills once again. Perhaps the uncertainty of Mother Nature lures the diehards who won't let a challenge lie by the wayside.

It was a cold, sub 30 degrees day with snow-covered park roads when Roy and I arrived. A park's truck spread sand, much to the appreciation of those early runners present. Hopes, too, were high for an accurate weather forecast prediction of sun and temperatures in the 40s for this day. The race directors held on to a positive, bright outlook as the field of runners grew.

As the hours slowly passed, we could bask in the sun's warmth and welcome less tenuous footage as the snow melted on the course. The race directors could smile that the Gods of Good Running Weather cast their blessings on the race this winter's day. Although quite a few runners signed up for the long haul, a total of 16 actually finished. However, many got a good hilly workout from doing any number of repeated 5K loops. Roy was pleased to complete four loops.

Roy and I used the course in preparation for the upcoming marathon and half marathon in Knoxville, TN where my youngest son, a youthful 38, will join me for the 26.2 miler. Of course, the dust he leaves behind will indicate his speedy leg turnover versus my turtle pace. When comparing our training notes, I related to him that this 50K would be my long training run, to which he replied, "Mom, that's not a long training run. That's insanity!" So much for youthful exuberance.

The repeat loops added up and my spirits were buoyed by encouragement from other runners, many of whom would lap me with their speed. My misery could not have been too bad as I came into the staging area announcing my loop completions with a smile. I really got a kick out of the smiley face sign at the turnaround point. For loops #5, #6, and #7, I lost my momentum, tiredness set in, and I started to think about this insanity thing. With renewed leg turnover, loops #8, #9, and #10 were better than expected. To finish in 5:47:13 and still feel good and smiling, it just doesn't get any better than this. Ironically, I was the 11th finisher, just as the columnist was in his race. I could have hugged the world. Those present got a big bear hug of appreciation. The trio of Roy and the two race directors got me to this incredible level of euphoria.

Although thoughts of retiring from ultra running did cross my mind, there just might be that spark relit next January when insanity take centers stage again, even in my older age.

The 50K Challenge

A day earlier it was a balmy 70 degrees. A day later the rain fell like a deluge. Sandwiched in between for the 50K race was a day unbelievably perfect for a January long run. It was about 40 degrees at the start and then near the low 50s for a while. It was a beautiful snowless morning. The race directors did not need the services of the park's sanding truck, as was the case in previous years.

"I think I'm young, so I act like it," someone once wrote. With that in mind and with a mending sore heel, I decided to try the 50K, doing one slow loop at a time. The sun warmed things up nicely, ideal weather for those who chose to run in shorts and short-sleeved tops. In short order, I removed my headband, rolled up my sleeves, and unzipped my jacket. Not wanting to further aggravate my Achilles tendon, I strongly harbored hopes of finishing the 50K, choosing to listen to my heart rather than my physical therapist's advice. Being ever persistent, I thought about these words of an unknown author: "The age factor means nothing to me. I'm old enough to know my limitations, and I'm young enough to exceed them."

Everyone seemed to be jovial, often conversing and laughing as they ran. So many cheered for me as we passed each other and so many speedsters lapped me. After about my fifth loop, a young woman going in the opposite direction yelled out, "Erika, you're awesome!" You can believe I sported the biggest smile ever. That woman runner, with her speed and fluid stride, was beauty in motion.

Many runners gave words of encouragement to another runner as he tackled the course several times. Another senior runner, recovering from a broken ankle and leg, valiantly completed six loops, some with Roy, who opted to conquer the hills with four loops. One ageless senior did several loops, then decided to run all the way home to Hyde Park. Amazing!

I eased into a slow comfort zone for six loops. An extra dose of Tylenol helped ward off potential heel pain, but did not stem the tide of aching quads. With three loops to go, I hoped for the repeat of my 2006 adrenaline high and good leg turnover. This was not to be as my vim, vigor, and vitality got lost by the wayside. Therefore, I continued at a snail's pace. Even my attempts to power-walk at times proved "oomphless." However, I've learned that you can keep going long after you think you can't. I willed myself to finish, which I did in 6:31:28, still smiling and still standing. This 2006 dynamo was the 2007 dud. Awaiting my arrival at the finish, in addition to Roy, were the two race directors and several long-staying volunteers. They all had enough time to get home for the football games on TV. I'm glad I didn't take any longer.

Toughing It Out at the 50K

Every year a dynamic duo spearhead the ever-challenging Recover from the Holidays 50K run. In recent years I have been crazy enough to further abuse my aged body by running all those unforgiving hills. Vowing never to do this again in one breath, I always get hyped up when the New Year dawns and this race is again listed.

Having a short-lived memory of last year's pain, I got psyched up to give it one more try in 2008. However, fate almost deemed otherwise. Leave it to me to be creative in getting injured, nearly dashing my hopes of running the course. On December 15th, while leaning over to put garbage in the dumpster, I lost my footing on the ice-covered snow mound and banged my chest on the dumpster's hard metal rim. Pain was minimal until three days later when my aching chest became unbearable. Lateral movements, walking, talking, coughing, sneezing, and taking deep breaths intensified the pain.

So, on December 18th, with Roy out on business, I slowly and painfully drove myself to my doctor's office, where the EKG showed no heart impairment. Then I drove back to our local hospital for prescribed X-rays, thankful that limited road traffic meant less upper body maneuvering. While being X-rayed, it hurt so much to inhale and stand in a rigid position that I felt dizzy, faint and got very sweaty (I was just hungry and so much in pain). The staff probably thought I was going into cardiac distress and quickly got me on a gurney for a trip to the emergency room, where I was put on a bed, hooked up to monitors (which I didn't need) and had an injection site port put in my arm.

I tried to tell everyone that my chest pain was from the fall, and echoing Roy's humor, told them the dumpster fared worse and they should see the big dent I left. After I cried buckets of tears, a wonderful RN came in with a cell phone to call Roy and injected me with a dose of morphine. In no time at all I was flying higher than a kite, giddy and smiling from ear to ear. My X-rays were then completed, Roy came to take me home, and I knew it was only a matter of time before euphoria would give way to more pain. Thank God the X-rays showed no fractures, only deep sternum contusions, with a recovery period of "several weeks" the nurse said. I told her, "I don't have several weeks!" Yet, how could I even consider running when walking was painful enough every time I took a deep breath?

On December 28th, I ventured outside for an easy walk with Roy and did the same the following three days. On January 1st, I gave it my all and ran 6.3 miles, the first pavement pounding in two and a half weeks. The discomfort was bearable and I followed this by another walk on January 3rd, two days before the BIG DAY. Still, the lingering question remained: Could I, should I consider running a 50K? Oh, how I prayed to God and willed myself to wellness.

Race day on January 5th, 2008 brought some slippery roads and cold temperatures as I and another runner opted for the early start. My plan was to do one loop at a time and take it from there. Despite some chest discomfort (along with a sore left quad, sore right Achilles tendon and pebbles in my shoes) I plodded on ever so slowly. The fact that I was always a bit ahead of that guy was my impetus not to quit. The race directors and the other volunteers were always so encouraging and Roy patiently waited with supplies after my every loop. At 6:36:17 I finished, about six minutes ahead of the guy I started with.

To accomplish something that seemed impossible for so many days is its own reward. To get a bear hug from Roy was the icing on the cake. I could not have done it without his love and support.

An Unfinished 50K

It was not my last hurrah, that's for sure. What inspired me to do the 50K for the past five years made me want to give it another try. A long layoff from running due to several injuries (gluteus muscles, hamstring and knee) did not afford me adequate time for long training runs. Heck, I was so glad when I could start pounding the pavement after many boring weeks of walking. Even a short run gave me many reasons to smile.

So, on January 3rd, it was time to test my mettle . . . or my sanity. With Roy's trepidation and my stubbornness, I decided to run as many loops as I could, hoping to do all ten, but realistically knowing the body might be in a rebellious mood much sooner. God bless a race director who was at the park already so I could get an early start. Even when the winds picked up on my fourth loop, I still held on to that glimmer of hope and got through it okay. I met my Waterloo on loop #5 when the winds were too formidable to fight and my pace greatly slowed. A quick mental calculation made me realize that I could probably finish in 3.5 plus more hours with a lot of walking. My first five loops already had taken more than three hours. I did not like the predicament I was in, nor did I want to risk injury and more downtime from running.

The decision I made was to be thankful for the 15.5 miles that I completed and do no more. It was not a time for heroics. I can't thank both race directors enough for their encouragement and for being out in the cold for me and all the other runners. Before I started, I told one that my injuries may not make it possible for me to finish the whole thing. He said, "That's okay." He was right. It was okay if I didn't finish the 50K. Yes, when it ended for me I was a bit sad, yet heartened that I did the best I could on that day at that time. There will be other long distances to conquer.

As I think about my long running journey, I am reminded of these words (author unknown): "If you have to ask the reason why I run, you wouldn't understand he answer."

Chapter Ten - Bring Back Pheidippides

"Only those who risk going too far can possibly find out how far they can go." – T. S. Eliot

Marathon Mania

In the crisp autumn weather runners often focus on marathons. So, in keeping with this quest, I wrote this poetic description of the journey that led to my first New York City Marathon in 1987.

My Yellow Brick Road to the Tour De Boroughs

My running started as a lark when I gave it a try,
I huffed and I puffed and I thought I would die.
My legs felt heavy and my pulse started to race,
I ran a 10K and won a first place.

The Rockland Half Marathon was run on a whim,
But it rained so hard that I wanted to swim.
Winter's chill paved the way for the summer's heat
While my injured leg felt like the agony of defeat.

I trained in the spring, in the summer and fall,
I had a big goal so I gave it my all.
My quads ached when I ran the "firehouse five."
The hills made me feel more dead than alive.

In the heat, in the rain, in the chill and the cold,
The pain was more than my legs could hold.
The miles added up and I did hill work too.

The "Doubting Georges" said that my mileage was too few.

My co-workers started a marathon collection,
And betted on the miles of their selection.
Would I go for it all or would I just place?
Would I stumble and fall and quit the big race?

I plodded on while the miles totaled more.
I ran a good race but boy, was I sore!
The blue line meandered as I entered Central Park.
To me it meant following the mark.

Up the hills and around the bend
I heard the cheers of many a friend.
The hill was all mine as the clock ticked away,
I ran under the banner -it sure made my day!

No more hours of running, no more endless miles,
I had my rose and medal and my face was all smiles.
My two oldest sons met me, their eyes filled with pride,
My emotions overtook me so I just sat down and cried.

I felt so euphoric and started to get giddy,
Knowing that I conquered the "boroughs of the city."
After running 26.2 miles I had passed the big test,
Now it was time to go home, and take a long rest

. . . and think about NEXT YEAR!

At the Finish Line

In the fall runners' thoughts often focus on the M word: MARATHONS. It's awesome autumn and murderous marathons incongruously blended into one. Spring fever has long since exited and marathon fever takes over. In short, the essence of fall is captured by the marathoning spirit. Soon winter will greet the runners but not before this one last hurrah.

In New York City, it is five boroughs spreading out their welcome mats and colorful banners that herald the onslaught of thousands of runners and the thunderous pounding of feet. As runners, we spend weeks and months going through our training runs. We eat, sleep, drink, and talk about what marathon(s) we hope to complete. SURVIVE is more like it! The main menu focuses on a pasta dish in one manner, shape, or form. To break the monotony, we eat pasta in colors of green and orange and shapes of pinwheels, shells, tubes, or whatever. It's that time again where training ends and THE BIG RACE takes over.

At our house a different twist is added to the word marathon. True, Roy and I diligently trained for the New York City "Tour de Boroughs," but it is my youngest son, Greg, who gives us a "run for our money." He leaves marathon messages on the answering machine! He doesn't run out of words until the beep comes on or the tape runs out. You might say that he reaches a different kind of finish line.

New York City Marathon Memories Times Three

1987 - My first marathon distance at age 49. Every inch of space at Fort Wadsworth was filled to the brim with runners. I felt so lost. Orphaned running clothes in a rainbow of colors decorated the trees and grass while medicinal scents permeated the air. After the start cannon went off, it took me a full nine minutes to get my feet moving in a forward direction. Biggest fans along the course were my two oldest sons. Their "HI MOM!" was music to my ears and helped me forget my sore and tired legs. At Columbus Circle my middle son suddenly bolted from the sidelines and started running alongside me, only to be sternly chased off the course by a policeman. "BUT SHE'S MY MOM!" he protested. This previously mentioned incident was such a morale booster for me. At the finish line my euphoria was so great that I almost grabbed my medal and rose from the hands of the race volunteers. My time: 4:48:59.

1988 - The theme could have been "You know it's a bad day when . . ." Stomach discomfort started on the bus ride to the bridge. My old standby remedy of Ritz crackers didn't work this time. A nauseous stomach protested my presence at the starting lineup. At 17 miles I "lost it." I tried to eat a banana only to watch it break apart in my hands and drop on the pavement. Was my stomach REALLY trying to tell me something? Central Park brought meager attempts at running amid walking, disorientation (why was the blue line so crooked?), and endless nausea. As I reached the finish line my nauseous stomach rebelled and I felt very cold. It was off to the medical tent! My time: 4:32:36.

1989 - Long lines at the portable toilets discouraged me from drinking any more water. French runners wearing comical green hats and international runners by the dozens converged on the island . . . a melting pot of runners and a potpourri of gaily-colored T-shirts. In Brooklyn I missed a much-needed water station and moaned. A man running near me suddenly handed me the rest in his cup. My heart pounded as the cup nearly dropped when I tried to reach for it. For a long time I ran behind a runner wearing a cap and gown. A marathon is infectious . . . somewhere behind me was my oldest son, twice a spectator but now running his first marathon. I sprinted the final upward climb to the finish line. My time: 4:04:12.

1990 - I CAN'T WAIT! A tradition has been born. This time my husband will be running his first "Tour de Boroughs."

I Run . . . Therefore I Ache

As a runner it's not always easy for me to overlook the disappointing aspects of less than desirable performances in my races. I compete too fiercely within myself. For instance, to come so close to nearly finishing a sub four-hour marathon and failing often gets the best of me. Okay, I'll put aside the 4:04 in New York City in '89 and the 4:03 (with a leg injury) in Dutchess County in '90, but I can't forget this past New York City Marathon which started out so well and ended so disappointingly. Feeling great, running strong, and reaching the 13.1 mile mark in 1:47:10 made me feel that "this was it." Forget about the pre-injured hamstring, I was on a roll and running for a PR (Personal Record).

Unfortunately the hamstring mercilessly gave out at mile 14 and two leg massages along the roadside only got me along another two miles. Then my OUCH got louder and more frequent. So it was a long 10 miles to the finish that I walked, hobbled and quasi-ran. Thanks to my oldest son, David, who met me at First Avenue and 68th Street and stayed with me until the final stretch, I was able to finish in 4:39:22.

Looking back is painful, like the hamstring injury. Yet I have to admit that I enjoyed the euphoria of "just being there." It was pain and pleasure incongruously blended. Roy keeps saying, "I KNOW you have a sub four-hour marathon in you." His words and the following quote are an inspiration: "Running is having a dream and making it come true." (Jane Dolley, from an article in the Road Runners Club of America

Footnotes, Winter 1991). So I'm off and running
... with a few pauses and many dreams along the way.

My Conquest of Big Sur

At the ungodly time of 2:37 AM the alarm clock blared and jolted Roy and me awake. In my state of semi-consciousness I blindly went through the motions of getting myself ready in time to leave the motel by four AM for the drive into Carmel and the 4:45 AM bus departure to Pfeiffer Big Sur State Park. While sitting in the rear of the bus my already nervous stomach took a beating while my facial complexion quickly attained that nauseous green look. Trying to dismiss any thoughts of getting sicker, I resorted to surveying the myriad types of footwear worn by the runners on the bus. Still, the question of "WHAT AM I DOING HERE?" always crept in. So I stared at more running shoes.

Amidst the fog, drizzle and darkness, it was 5:30 AM when the bus reached the park's staging area. The lines to the porta-toilets quickly resembled winding strings of spaghetti entwined many times over. There was no end . . . EVER! About 12 minutes before the race was scheduled to start I got my last turn. As they so humorously did, the guys started their "timing." You better believe that I was not going to sit and contemplate!

The gun went off at exactly seven o'clock AM, heralding the start of the marathon as some 2,400 runners headed for the hills of Big Sur. Fog was slowly rising through the trees and valleys, soon to give way to scenic wonders. The race route meandered up and down mostly along the Pacific Coast Highway. Early into the run a downpour drenched me for about 30 minutes. By the time I got to mile 10 and the start of the two mile, 520 foot climb to Hurricane Point, the warm sun that then prevailed not only dried my clothes but added glistening highlights to the mystical beauty of the surroundings. About a mile into the climb both of my knees started aching. I knew that the 40 foot to 560 foot ascent would take its toll, but not this quickly.

As the upward climb continued, I chuckled at the humorous Burma-Shave signs along the roadside. After reaching the top (one sign said, "Look back at where you have been") the downhill portion was a blessing for my aching quads and I reveled at the awesome sights and sounds that surrounded me. My eyes were treated to the majestic beauty of tall, rugged-edged mountains and magnificent ocean scenes while my ears were caressed by the ever-present sounds of roaring ocean waves. Truly a delight to the senses. Along the route several orchestras played their tunes of encouragement. It was quite a sight to see musicians in their fancy attire high above the sea at overlooks with views enough superlatives can't describe. Walkers joined the runners for a seven mile stretch and offered endless words of encouragement. A common experience of pain and determination seemed to bind us all together.

On and on I ran, stopping at porta-toilets perching high on the cliffs and drinking all the fluids I could handle, while my quads continued their own agonizing rebellion. No sooner did I finish one hill when another appeared on the horizon. I began to mutter aloud to no one in particular words like "Darn these hills" and "My legs can't take it any longer" and "WHAT AM I DOING HERE?" After mile 14 I somehow "lost" Roy when he slowed to massage a painful Charley Horse and I unknowingly continued onward. The portable toilets became scarcer after the 15th mile. One guy was so kind as to direct me to a steep path in the bushes off a cliff, an offer I not so kindly declined.

The miles were marked by large wooden fiddle-shaped signs so I played a game of running from fiddle to fiddle. Shortly before the finish line a beautiful beach area with glistening white sand and blue-green water appeared on my left. Reluctantly I dismissed the desire to soothe my aching hot feet. I felt engulfed by euphoria when I finally passed mile 26 and saw the flashing lights of the finish line in the distance. As if hit by a sudden burst of energy, I began sprinting to those flashing lights. Closer and closer . . . soon I was under the clock. I had survived the arduous and challenging Big Sur Marathon. I was a Hurricane Point survivor.

Only after I had stopped running did I realize how sore I really was. Walking was an ordeal and getting up from a sitting position was a near impossibility. Everywhere I looked, runners were walking funny and I, too, was one of many among the "walking wounded." Despite this, I wore a smile that stretched from ear to ear. For one day Roy and I, like so many others, had conquered the mighty Big Sur. It was truly the agony of de feet, de knees, de legs, and de arms all incongruously blended in with the thrill of conquest.

Capture the Marathon Spirit

THE MARATHON SPIRIT - a feeling that dominates the fall running scene. I know that I had taken on quite a challenge when I signed up for back-to-back "Warwick" marathons. The first one was the Ocean State Marathon in Rhode Island, traversing the route from Narragansett to Warwick. The second one was the inaugural Warwick (New York) Marathon one week later.

The temperature rose quickly with a brilliant sun filling the sky for the former. By the time the Rhode Island marathon started, an over-abundance of hot sunshine prevailed. The course route was all out in the open, devoid of trees and shade, making the sun's rays feel even hotter as I ran. Sea breezes were negligible.

I was on pace for the first half. However, the hot sun and resulting dehydration took its toll. I am not a hot weather runner. Therefore, with dizziness and weak legs, I dropped out at 16 miles. My heart wanted me to continue running, yet I knew my mind had to rule that day. If some days are diamonds and some days are stone, then this definitely was a stone day.

Many trepidations prevailed as I awaited the start of the inaugural Warwick (New York) Marathon during a heavy downpour. Not knowing anything about the course except that this area was known to be very hilly made my heart do flip-flops.

The race director had promised to change some of the course's hilly sections and I secretly hoped that he had. Although the day was a bit warm and humid, a gentle rainfall kept things cooler while overcast skies hid the sun, protecting the runners from its direct hot rays.

The first four miles were "very forgiving" and I enjoyed the surrounding countryside. A short time later there were some hilly projections and more great scenery as the course weaved its way through the communities of Amity, Pine Island, and Florida (New York).

I was amazed at the many cheering spectators on the roadside and enjoyed the uplifting music to run by that resounded at several locations along the route. The community spirit was wonderful and gave me a warm inner glow.

Shortly after passing the 18th mile, I caught up with a pair of runners who warned me about the "bad hills between 19 and 23 miles." How bad could they be, I thought to myself.

Well, The hills WERE there and they ALL went forever upward. Downhills didn't seem to be of equal length. The "killer hill" came at the 24th mile. It was very, very steep. When I saw this hill approaching, I looked upward in search of the pearly gates of heaven. All I could say was "Oh, my God, you gotta be kidding!" A voice seemed to say, "No, He is not kidding." And He wasn't! This definitely was a hill to power-walk. I thought I was doing another Mt. Washington run-up!

The final home stretch seemed never ending. Was there ever going to be an easy way to the finish line? Although my body and legs were exhausted, my mind and spirit remained strong in my resolve to finish, which I finally did in 3:54:57.

Later, as I proudly clutched my finisher's medal, I recalled its inscription: "Pride lasts longer than pain." After all, isn't that what marathoning is all about?

A Great Marathon in the Smoky Mountains

It sounded very intriguing. I first heard about the Smoky Mountain Marathon while Roy and I were on vacation, touring through several states. A runner who we met at a motel in rural Kentucky related that it's a "must" for all marathon runners. Thus a dream was born.

Inquiries to and information from the host club, the Knoxville (Tennessee) Track Club, followed. I applied in early December, 1996 and motel accommodations in Townsend, Tennessee were quickly confirmed. It was then more than a two and a half month wait during which time I could only squeeze in one long 17 mile run. Would my marathon savvy be enough and would my running legs not fail me?

As careful as l was to keep injury-free, the unexpected happened. What happened to me was just dumb luck. One of our cats overturned the garbage can. It was the Persian with half a face and half a brain. He's named Perdue, but certainly not after the distinguished university, rather, more like the chicken. In trying to scoot him away I slipped on the linoleum floor with the last two right-foot toes separating around the cornered wall. OUCH!!! I yelled at the cat (a lot of good THAT did) and screamed out in pain. In no time at all the affected area was swollen and took on a multitude of colors. Was it broken? Why now? Why less than eight days before this important race? Was this going to be the "agony of de feet or defeat?"

Although X-rays revealed no fractures the toe and foot remained painfully swollen. To help me get beyond the

20 mile mark my podiatrist skillfully taped the injured area, making it more stable and to ease the discomfort of running on it.

My earlier concerned questions about running the race were answered on Saturday, February 22nd, the day of the 24th Annual Smoky Mountain Marathon. Of course, I had the usual pre-race jitters and a very nervous stomach. While temperatures in the warm 70s prevailed earlier in the week, a strong wind and rainstorm passed through the area the day before. Weather forecasters warned of a cold front and gusty winds enroute for race day. On race day temperatures were in the 40s with the wind chill bringing them down to about 30 degrees. Winds hovered around 25 MPH with higher gusts. A sharp drop in temperature was predicted.

The race began in the center of Townsend, a quiet country village affectionately known as the "peaceful side of the Smokies." The previous day's storm left debris on the roads and we were advised to proceed with caution and be vigilant at certain areas along the course. Disaster nearly struck me when I twisted my left ankle while trying to run over the crushed remnants of a tree limb. I hobbled a bit, put weight on the foot and slowly continued to run again. Whew! This could have been a runner's worst nightmare. Was I flirting with fate or what?

The turnaround point at two and a half miles was at the entrance to the Smoky Mountain National Park. What beautiful scenery! The course then followed the base of the mountains as we headed north on scenic Route 321 where strong headwinds buffeted the runners. At seven and a half miles we crossed over the Little River and entered a park area where a winding course and rolling hills prevailed. The toughest hills came between 18 and 22 miles, mostly on a dirt and gravel type roadbed.

All along the course the runners were so friendly and volunteers shouted encouragement. This made me feel good inside. I forgot about the "outside" pain. We laughed about bucking the strong headwinds that were so energy draining. Remember, this is country running and Southern Appalachian scenery at its best.

At 19.5 miles, where "the wall" tends to meet the runners, there was a guy dressed as a sheriff and a life-size cardboard cutout of Roy Rogers holding his two six-guns. Here many of the runners got stamped with stickers depicting a good luck horseshoe. This was a lively spot, for sure, and suitably called OK Corral. It was here that Roy met me with fresh liquid replacement and a lot of "Lookin' good, kiddo." This spot heralded the beginning of the end, i.e. the last 10K-plus to the finish and back to the center of the village. There were more rolling hills to contend with. A welcomed long downhill was like manna from heaven.

After traversing the Little River again and with less than two miles to go the end was nearly in sight. With each approaching footstrike I could hear the excitement at the finish line. It was music to my ears.

As each runner approached the last turn his or her arrival was announced, first by bib number, then by name and hometown. I was greeted with, "and here comes runner number 18, with long blond hair and nice long legs." This really cracked me up. Had I heard that at 19 miles my boosted ego would have lifted me so far off the ground that I would have reached the finish line banner in record time. You better believe I was smiling broadly for the cameraman! The clock showed 4:17:12, good enough for second place in the 50 plus age group, losing first place by a mere 35 seconds. I was thrilled.

For runners who like the small town hospitality and some of the most beautiful scenery east of the Mississippi, this race is for you. It certainly gave my running legs a workout, but the memories of having done it will last for a long, long time.

The Warwick Marathon (A Day for Heroes)

For the average person it was an average day. For the Warwick Marathon runners it was a special day dedicated to a special cause with each and every participant running it for his or her own special reason. For a cancer patient named Darren and all those who persevered and crossed the finish line it was a day to be a hero. A day to proclaim, "Yes, I did it!"

For me, like my fellow marathon runners, it was a day to bask in the glory of being a marathon runner. Of feeling the pain as the miles crept up. Of watching a brave young man reach the finish line with the cheers (and tears) of a welcoming crowd greeting him in this moment of triumph.

This fall classic marathon had everything including beautiful scenery with autumn's palette of colors of gold, orange, yellow and red. It had crisp cool temperatures, an abundance of enthusiastic spectators, signs along the route welcoming all the runners, music to run in tune with (and even do a quick dance step to), fantastic volunteers, and water stops laden with replenishing fluids. The many water stations were manned by energetic children and adults, members of the Boy Scouts and Girl Scouts, and members of the community. If anything was in abundance throughout the day it was the community spirit. You heard it, you saw it, you felt it, you lived it.

I ran for redemption because the flu knocked me out of the 1996 event. Darren ran because he had two goals for 1997: to beat his cancer and to run the arduous 26.2 miles. He believed that uphill battles with cancer and uphills on the course were beatable. His goal was to conquer both. How well he succeeded in his victories!

My emotions ran the spectrum from tiredness and anxiety to laughter and tears of joy. At the starting lineup I felt the butterflies in my stomach and the momentary weakness in my legs. Once on the road it was the agony of de feet, de body, de legs, and de arms. I was determined not to succumb to the agony of defeat.

For me it was playing mind games as the long miles dragged on. It was admiring the foliage and for a fleeting moment or two wishing I was playing in a pile of cushioning leaves.

By the time I reached mile 18 my legs lost their cooperative nature. I plodded along, mile after endless mile, thankful for all the volunteers and spectators. Thankful, too, to catch glimpses of my husband as he rode the course on his bicycle, always offering words of encouragement and support. I didn't dare tell him the many times I considered dropping out because my exhausted body craved sleep. Neither he nor the others would let me stop.

I commiserated with other runners as we ran side by side. After a while I even offered encouraging words to several first time marathon runners. This helped me to stay focused also. One was suffering from leg cramps, another from blistered toes, and a third, named Chris, was flip-flopping positions with me. We played a game of runner's leap frog. I marveled at how strong Chris looked as she reeled in the miles. Her mother would be waiting for her at the finish. Somehow we both knew in our hearts that we would finish. That we would be a hero for a day.

The last mile seemed to take forever. Chris and I thought we'd never see the finish line banner. Yet there it was, just around the corner. Chris erred briefly by entering the wrong chute, giving me a chance to kick it in. One second separated our finishing times. A handsome young lad put a finisher's medal around my neck, then around the neck of Chris. We were both home free. Our long running journey was over.

My husband had to bicycle another seven miles back to the start to get the car, while I stayed behind with the other finishers. The spectators and volunteers continued their enthusiastic cheers as each runner's journey climaxed at the finish line. A volunteer for the day allowed me the chance to sit in his van and stay warm.

My spirits peaked again when the announcement came that runner Darren was on West Street. I would see a true hero finish. I would witness the strength of prayer and of one's spirit and faith. The air was filled with cheers and applause when Darren appeared, escorted by two running buddies, all crossing the finish line together. His time did not matter. The magnitude of this feat told it all. I think we all felt a part of Darren's victory, even those of us who didn't know him personally.

I thought of the song from Hercules called "Go the Distance" and of my finishing time of 4:11:25. I also thought of all the runners who achieved a personal goal and succeeded in going the distance. I thought of the race director's words: "This is your day; as you stand at the start facing the challenge, know that today you are a hero!"

This was the 1997 Warwick Marathon.

The Musical Beat of the Feet

It was an inaugural event, this first Country Music Marathon in downtown Nashville, Tennessee. My youngest son Greg, who lives in Tennessee, and I decided to "go for it" and signed up early for this April 29, 2000 event. This would be Greg's debut into the world of marathoning. Greg was able to do some long runs up to 17 miles, usually finishing the second half in negative splits. I knew I was in for some tough competition despite my previous 23 marathons and several ultras. When I was ready to start my longer training runs my casted left arm from a broken wrist negated this. Seven weeks took its toll and even with the heavy cast I could only get up to a 10 miler. Then time ran out and rest and hydration were in order. Still, we both felt that we just had to believe in our dream of finishing the marathon.

With a scheduled starting time of 7 AM we had to get up at the ungodly hour of 3:45 AM, then leave an hour later for the drive to Nashville. Nerves were in full swing. Bathroom trips were many. Roy drove us, along with my twin sister, to the start at downtown Centennial Park. He then parked the car at the finish, Adelphia Coliseum, across the city.

At Centennial Park the sun rose quickly giving birth to a bright new dawn. Runners and porta-toilets were too numerous to count. Signs for designated areas were visible and baggage "cars," UPS trucks, were neatly lined up. The starting corrals were well marked. So many volunteers!

With Amy Grant at the microphone, singer Vince Gill shot off the gun for the start. I had moved back to be with Greg in his assigned corral so that we could start together. Later, an aerial view showed the start to be thousands of bobbing heads filling the streets of downtown Nashville. Moving forward was a slow process. Greg was really psyched up. Soon after the start his exuberance became evident when he raised his arms and shouted, "One-fifth of a mile!"

At about the three mile mark I knew it was not going to be my day for running. Greg raced on ahead. The early morning mid-40 temperatures quickly gave way to warmer sunshine, too hot for my lycra tights which soon became pedal-pushers. I quickly lost sight of Greg and concentrated on the festive atmosphere of the marathon. The course was lined with many musical bands and singers. Truly music to keep the feet moving. The course took runners past the famous Grand Old Opry House, past energetic cheerleaders at virtually every mile, and past the sights and sounds of Nashville.

The route was undulating and hillier than expected. It was quite a rude awakening that Nashville is not flat. At mile 20 Roy met me, saying Greg was eight to nine minutes ahead. Hyped spectators continued their encouraging cheers. Lord knows I needed all the help I could get!

At mile 21 trouble began for me as my body was quickly fading, calling for run-walk segments between miles 22 and 25, with cramping calves the norm. Then, with adrenaline kicking in at mile 25, I ran one of my fastest 1.2 miles ever. Yet I could not pass Greg. He ran a great 4:29:34 for his marathon debut. His ever-lovin' mother was less than 3 minutes behind in 4:32:29, good enough for 3rd place in the 60-64 age group. We both finished with a wonderful dose of memories . . . and sore feet!

Another Country Music Marathon, Nashville, Tennessee: April 28, 2001

This year's Country Music Marathon was a test of one's own fortitude. The course through Nashville is so open and unshaded. With the temperature reaching 82 degrees, I felt like a fried omelet on the scorching pavement. By mile 11 I was ready to call it quits. A runner from California told me not to drop out but to go "one mile at a time." I ignored my stomach problems and followed his advice . . . and finished!!!

My son Greg beat me by a whopping 35 minutes, finishing with a chip time of 4:05 to my 4:40. Yet I was not alone in my misery with the heat as some 1,000 runners dropped out. I even placed second in my age group, 60-64. Thank God I continued to put one foot in front of the other until I reached the finish line. Looking every bit as bad as I felt, I was shocked to learn that I was interviewed and shown on local TV. Egads! It must have been a horror show then.

A Review of Two Marathons: Nashville and Vermont

I ran these two marathons for different reasons. It was my third time (out of its four years) for the Country Music Marathon (April 26) and my first time for the Vermont City Marathon in Burlington (May 25). I am committed to run the Nashville one with my youngest son every other year now as long as he reciprocates to run The Turkey Trot 25K every other year. I had never done the Vermont City Marathon and relatives there prodded me to run in their hometown.

The Fitness Expos for both were good and interesting but very crowded. Race packet pick-up was easy, fast, and well organized for both. Nashville added a half marathon two years ago (same start time) while Vermont had more than 600 multiple-person relay teams along with individual runners (also same start time). Registration closed out quickly.

Nashville uses its Centennial Park, which boasts a full scale replica of the Parthenon, for equipment checking with assigned UPS trucks – "See what Brown Can do for you . . ." This is also used for the starting area. Battery Park is the gathering and starting area for Vermont. Tagged, bagged items were randomly placed in a pavilion there for transporting to the finish. Only runners were allowed in Centennial Park, whereas family members and friends could and did accompany race participants at Vermont's Battery Park. I was happy that Roy could keep me company and save places for me on the porta-toilet lines. No tents were available for the morning's rain. However, a Dunkin' Donuts stand offered free coffee along with a great plastic poncho. Nashville had a picnic pavilion but no rain! A real disappointment was the lack of toilet paper at all the toilet facilities in Nashville's park. From earlier experiences I recalled that there was a shortage of this item. Roy and I came prepared. My son used the newspaper he was reading. He had no other takers!

The courses are different.

Nashville has rolling hills and its many exposed areas get very hot with the sun. There are about two dozen bands, spirited high school cheerleading squads, and areas of cheering spectators along the way. A mile-long incline begins the final 6.2 miles and runners pass the Adelphia Coliseum where the finish line is. So close and yet so far away. The killer hills come at about mile 22.5 in beautiful Shelby Park.

Burlington has too many turns. We ran some streets a second time and ran under the START banner several times. The treelined residential neighborhoods were nice but had so many sharp turns. The closed-to-traffic Beltway section was less hectic as was the first short stretch on the city's south side bike path. The course was mostly flat with a steep hill at about mile 15 back at Battery Park, where there were many cheering crowds, followed by rolling terrain. The final four miles were on a paved, scenic bike path alongside Lake Champlain. A convoluted finish line area was at Waterfront Park.

Both marathons offered many energetic spectators and volunteers. Somehow, I like to run on the many rural roads of the Dutchess County Classic Marathon. For a smaller-scale event it also offers a half marathon and a

5K race. There are more than enough amenities and volunteers. The DC Classic is a well-organized event and it is local.

Note: Due to multiple traffic control issues and decreased participation, the DC Classic Marathon was discontinued after the 2007 event.

The Inaugural Trigon Bay Bridge Marathon: A Run Across the Chesapeake Bay Bridge-Tunnel

It was the night before the big race. The rhythm of the ocean's waves against the seashore did not lull me to sleep as I had hoped. Thus, my adventure started on a dark October morning at the ungodly hour of 1:30 AM when our hotel's wake-up call came in error and made me jump out of bed. My anxious and tired body got only about two and a half hours of sleep.

About 35 busses arrived early at the pick-up area for boarding at 4 AM. I positioned myself in the rear of the bus next to the restroom. Of course!! Doors closed at 4:50 AM and the caravan began the long drive across the span to the starting point near the opposite shore. Although I had the whole seat to myself I could not doze as some people did. The drive seemed endless. As the miles passed I envisioned the miles we would all soon be running.

We arrived at the assigned spot near the starting area at about 6:30 AM, with most of us choosing to remain in place rather than venture out in the dark with the gusty winds. The lines to the restroom on the bus were long, a testimony to everyone's apprehensions and nerves. At about 6:50 AM I exited the bus to join the line up at the start. A helicopter hovered overhead while police boats patrolled the waters below. As if to release pre-race energy we all waved at the helicopter. So much pumped-up energy from so many raised arms.

The 7:00 AM start was very orderly with a magnificent sunrise visible in the still darkened and overcast skies.

Very gusty headwinds prevailed. Since more than half of the race traversed the bridge-tunnel the strong winds were an ever-present foe. Oh, my aching arms! It was comforting to know that I was not alone in my battle with the headwinds.

Runners passed me, I passed runners, we flip-flopped positions, all the while sharing our desire to reach terra firma at 14.5 miles. While the open span was windy and cool, the two tunnels were surprisingly quite warm. Traffic occupied one lane in the tunnels while the other lane was for the runners. The air quality was acceptable although I did smell fumes at times.

The tunnels had about a three percent uphill grade before exiting on the span again. The respite that they offered from the wind was all too brief. The view from the span couldn't be overlooked. The shore that once seemed so far away soon became a reality. It was uplifting to be cheered on by so many spectators after leaving the span.

Somewhere near mile 18 or 19 a guy about half my age asked me if I wanted to "sprint to the finish" with him. Did my now slower gait indicate I was a sprinter? I think not! My terse but pleasant reply was, "You gotta be kidding. Do these legs look like they are sprinting?" Off he went into the wild blue yonder. I chuckled. Me? Sprint to the finish?

I started alternating running and walking and dreaming of going to sleep. Boy, was I tired! I flipped-flopped positions with so many runners that it became a game of leap frog for us. In between our tiredness and slower pace we were able to joke about our situation because we couldn't even gain speed on the remaining level and downhill areas. Roy met me at mile 23 and kept me company. He sure had more vim, vigor, and vitality than I did! With one mile to go I reached the concrete boardwalk along the beach for the final stretch. The finish line banner and clock came closer and closer. It was my last hurrah, running my fastest mile and overtaking a runner in front of me. The clock showed 4:40:42. Although I felt very good my tired body begged for some zzzs.

Food! We were treated to a welcomed chicken barbeque in the park near the beach. The awards ceremony followed at 6:00 PM. Bill Rodgers was there as the winners were presented their awards. How thrilled I was to place first in the 60-64 age group and be personally congratulated by him. I was surprised to learn that my nearest competitor was 22 minutes behind me.

This was one superbly organized and safe event. It made us pioneers by being the first to run a marathon across the waters of the Chesapeake Bay.

Boston Remembered

I never thought I'd want to relive the '93 Boston Marathon with its slow congested start, blazing hot sun beating down on me, and the high temperatures that made completing it a "Himalayan Conquest." When Alberto Salazar finished signing my bib number at the Expo the day before, his words of wisdom to me were "Run it to complete it." He could have said "Run it, walk it, crawl it," because I felt like doing all three at various times.

Along the 26.2 mile course I always managed to follow and/or catch up to two male runners whose T-shirts carried humorous words. One simply said THE MAC ATTACK and I kept thinking of a Big Mac hamburger being devoured or the runner being so hungry that he would attack anything vaguely resembling a Big Mac. I don't think he found his golden arches that day! Fallen arches, perhaps. The other runner's shirt was more to the point: BRIDGET TALKED ME INTO DOING THIS. Seeing him struggle to walk at times, I had the feeling he was not thinking kind thoughts of Bridget. Her words probably haunted him the entire 26.2 long miles.

The best, by far, was the T-shirt worn by a female runner. Following her, runners could read BEST BUNS IN BOSTON. That gal sure has a lot of spirit!

Why I Ran the 2004 Richmond Marathon

I like the challenge of a long distance run, especially the marathon. Combine this with having lived in Richmond from 1941 to 1948 and it is easy to understand why running along the streets of my childhood appealed to me. In addition, there was also an 8K race, ideal for Roy since he usually just waits and waits during those long hours that I am on the marathon course somewhere. Hence a trip to Virginia for the SunTrust Richmond Marathon last November was made. Nostalgia must have been an impetus.

Although I returned there in 1955 and again in 2002, the changes were enormous from the former trips and now. According to the course map, we would run some familiar streets and pass by or near sights of those bygone years. To me, running this marathon was akin to coming home. I really wanted to return to my southern roots.

On the evening of our arrival, Montezuma's Revenge greeted me and I got very little sleep. Upon awakening the next morning, the Gods of Bad Weather reigned. A steady, cold downpour prevailed. Confusion took over when we were given poor directions to the host hotel and spent one and a half hours driving around, trying to figure out where to go. Finding the parking garage at the host hotel was a lesson in futility. We opted for whatever was available and found a church's garage with very tiny spaces. We figured we needed the blessings from above.

From there we got more directions and walked in the rain to the site of the Runners Expo to pick up our race packets and chips. We quickly left and visited a site memorable to my youth which is now designated as a historic preservation landmark.

After dinner, we returned to our hotel room to settle our nerves and prepare for the next day's races. Methodically we assembled our outfits, affixed the chip, filled our hydration bottles, and put out bananas and juice for an early breakfast in our room. Panic set in when we couldn't find our bib numbers. It was now 7:30 PM and the Expo closed at 9 PM. I was nearly in tears and Roy was equally upset. I again examined and thoroughly scrutinized my chip packet envelope. There tightly tucked against the side face side hidden from view was a sheet the same size as the envelope. It was my precious bib number. Ditto for Roy's. We could breathe a big sigh of relief.

On race day morning we left our hotel at 5:50 AM in hopes of using the large parking garage at the host hotel in downtown Richmond. I took a generic Imodium and we tried to calm our frazzled nerves while waiting for the 8 AM marathon start. The 8K start was at 8:45 AM and two blocks away so Roy had time to stay with me. It was cold and windy. The humidity was a high 93 percent and the temperature hovered near 40 degrees. Soon I left Roy behind and started my long running journey. I passed sites and scenes from my childhood, ran along the famous Monument Avenue where my sisters and I played as youngsters, and ran near the street where our old house still stands. So many emotions. I passed Byrd Park where I played so many years ago. In the later stages of the race, I ran near the now historic Sacred Heart Cathedral Church which I attended decades ago.

The winds were so strong, at times approaching 30 MPH. I stayed with a group of runners who were going at my pace. It was cold along the James River, windy on the bridges and gusty in other areas, especially at about mile 15. We seemed to run on more concrete in the later stages, on highways that didn't exist during my time there. At about 18 miles, my legs started to talk back. I didn't like what I was hearing or my rapidly stiffening quads. A young runner in front of me had these words on the back of her T-shirt: "What was I thinking 20 weeks ago?" I chuckled, passed her, and tried to keep going forward with a depleted energy level.

Elation started to overtake me when the course returned to the downtown area and I knew that I was going to finish. A left turn onto Cary Street and then about ten blocks to go. I sprinted on the downhill and passed three runners. I saw Roy in the distance, waving his arms and cheering me in. I did it! My chip time was 4:48:57. Placing first (65 and over).

Running this race: Challenging
Returning to my roots: Priceless

Boston '04 – A Battle with the Sun

The Gods of Running bowed to the weatherman and a heat wave engulfed runners at the Hopkinton noontime start. The long wait at Athletes' Village was over as I wilted in the sun's rays while waiting in my assigned corral. Nearly 17 minutes later, I reached the start, long after two fighter jets did a flyover to herald the 108th running of the Boston Marathon.

After running only 1K, I knew it would not be a day for heroics. I think the predicted forecast of 30 MPH tailwinds was just an appeasement to diminish the impending high temperatures. The former did not materialize. The heat was too intense and I decided to forego time and use strategy for reaching the finish line without suffering leg cramps or dehydration. Dropping out was not an option. Since I tended to overheat quickly as I ran when my body's core temperature spiked, walking became a big part of the equation. By a combination of running and walking, I hoped that the heat would not get the best of me. Roy later told me that the thermometer on his backpack soared to over 90 degrees at the top of Heartbreak Hill while he awaited my arrival. However, I was so far behind my scheduled arrival time that he left before I got there, fearing that I had been brought to a medical tent.

It was HOT! Never had I seen so many runners in medical distress or so many runners walking in a marathon. Scores of ambulances traversed the course route, defeated runners sat by the curbside while others were on stretchers and covered with mylar blankets. Participants dropped like flies. Buses were seen taking fallen warriors back to the finish in Boston. Opened fire hydrants gave a gentle spray of cold water as did a multitude of hoses and lawn sprinklers set up along the roadway. My slower pace allowed me to meet so many nice people along the way. If misery loves company, I was in good hands. Some of us could even laugh at our plight. We were going nowhere in a hurry so it was a mutual admiration society.

The miles passed ever so slowly. The open areas were hotter than hell. I was determined to ward off leg cramps even if I had to ease up on running. My legs certainly were not in their glory this day. After reaching the designated mile 21 marker, I saw no other mile or kilometer indicators on the long stretch along Commonwealth Avenue. This was disheartening since I had no idea where I was. All I kept hearing from the crowd was "You're almost there" and "Only one mile to go." I knew that was not true.

After what seemed like an eternity, I got onto Boylston Street and I could see the finish line area in the distance. I charged onward with renewed energy. The clock said 6:07-something and the temperature reading was 83 degrees now. I had conquered the heat and hills. While my skin was white as snow at the start, I was now a crispy critter. Bright red is not my favorite color. Later, I learned that my official chip time was 5:51:14, by far my slowest marathon to date, but one of my most rewarding ones. My finisher's medal is a cherished keepsake.

"The man who knows it can't be done counts the risk, not the reward." - Elbert Hubbard

The Marathon With an Ouch!

Dreams don't die. They are just rescheduled. I had to take a dream detour at the Dutchess County Classic Marathon.

The weather on race day was a runner's delight. I felt real good, well rested and "ready to roll." Pacing myself for the first half went well. It didn't matter who was in front of or behind me. I even stopped to talk to a course marshal about a serious safety issue I noticed earlier when a defiant runner chose not to run on the designated safe roadside areas. Time lost didn't matter.

As I later learned, life is what happens when you make other plans. I met Roy at the midpoint, left him with my empty hydration bottle, and continued on my merry way, still on track for a sub-4:40 finishing time. Shortly after mile 14, all plans went awry.

I suddenly found myself landing hard on the gritty, sandy roadway. Certainly not a graceful landing, more like a frontal PLOP! My chin hit the surface so hard that I thought my jaw was broken. Road rash was painful. Pebbles and sand aren't too nutritious. Roy would later claim that the highway department would charge me for the big dent that I left in the roadway.

With the help of a traffic control person, I got up, put weight on my legs, and decided to try running. Talk about "rolling with the punches." For me it was mind over matter. The course marshals probably thought that I lost my mind. I think I left them behind with looks of disbelief as I continued running.

Being somewhat of a bloodied mess, I kept going, albeit slower, with the hope that as long as I could put one foot in front of the other, I'd continue to do so. Despite the discomfort with each footstrike, it was not a reckless or foolish decision. Rather it was based on knowing my body and its limitations. If I had to quit, I would have. Well, maybe . . .

I did a lot of talking to myself for reassurance. The ambulance crew and some course personnel wanted me to stop and be medically checked. An object in motion stays in motion, right? Therefore, I told them all that "I may be old and I may be slow but I am still moving forward and am NOT stopping."

A cyclist accompanied me for the last two miles or so, being my Guardian Angel on a bike. She knew I was on a mission to finish what I started nearly five hours earlier. Several times I had to stop dead in my tracks due to the curvy road with no shoulder and speeding vehicles. In due time I remember seeing Roy, the EMTs, and the large finish line banner. When I stopped, I hugged a friend, telling her "I really hurt."

The EMTs finally had their race casualty to administer aid to. I could later smile when the earlier word that was sent out mentioned an injured 35-year-old runner. What a morale booster, especially for a 69-year-old pushing 70!

Although at 4:59:18 I missed my dream time, there was so much to smile about. The cheering, enthusiastic hydration station kids, the countless volunteers, the people on the course who wanted to help, the fantastic traffic control/course marshal crew, and finally for me finishing and being able to say, "I DID IT!" I recall these words from a roadside sign in Maine: "Never regret anything that made you smile." I certainly have no regrets.

To Be or Not to Be : A Selfish Runner Speaks Out

In a club newsletter a runner wrote: "Running a marathon is a selfish thing to do." This is my response to this challenging statement.

Yes, running a marathon can be considered a selfish thing to do. However, let's examine its need to be so categorized. I question which action is really at the core of being selfish.

It is selfish because it is something only the runner can do for himself or herself. It is selfish because, in taking on the monumental task of running a marathon, the runner must put aside a special block of time devoted solely to this goal. To do less would be an open invitation to failure. I now ask: Is it selfish to pursue a personal goal? If so, then I consider being selfish a virtue.

I find fault with the mindset that believes that anyone who puts his or her needs first is labeled as selfish. Don't we, as individuals and as runners, count at all? Can't we put aside or put on hold for a short time the daily consuming responsibilities of doing for others in place of doing for ourselves? Can't the average runner dare to dream a bit more, shine a bit brighter or strive for excellence as a runner? Can't we be true to that inner voice that says "go for it," whatever "it" may be?

I believe the runner is selfish only in what he or she must give up in order to reach this high achievement goal. For instance, this runner must give up the luxury of a warm home to go out and train in all kinds of inclement weather. This runner must be selfish enough to stick to a commitment without giving in to the whims of nature, the tired feelings of an overworked on-the-job body, and the many demands of family (and personal) responsibilities. This runner must be selfish enough to sacrifice comfort, overlook the "easy way out," and take to the high road. While the family can nestle around a warm fireplace in the cold of winter and take to the water in the heat of summer, this runner must brace the elements of nature or let a running dream die by the wayside. Who is really selfish here, I ask?

As for me, I believe and feel that I am entitled to be selfish and do something for myself. My running goals represent a personal commitment. In no way are my other commitments diminished. After years of doing for others and family, I have earned the privilege of doing something for myself. Believe me, a single parent can rarely put herself or himself first. Therefore, having been short-changed on the yardstick of leisure time, I am now ready and able to pursue more personal growth through running marathons and long distance events.

My question is this: Am I selfish because I run and I train and perhaps take time away from or inconvenience others or am I selfish when I short-change my time and goals for the sake of others? Am I selfish at their expense or at my expense?

If running a marathon is really a selfish thing to do, then why does the popularity of "going the distance" continue? What a wonderful and fulfilling way to be selfish! Don't tear apart the dreams and hopes of future marathoners by calling them selfish. I say "more power to them." I like running with all these selfish people. They are happier, healthier, and a very nice bunch.

My Response to Marathon Mania

As a veteran of 34 marathons and 8 ultras to date, I found the article titled Marathon Mania to be demeaning and elitist. The words were less than inspiring or encouraging to any regular, average, and proud finisher or hopeful finisher, and offensive to any runner, fast or slow, who has ever gone the distance. This includes myself, a mere "rank amateur" according to the author's standards and whose marathons he describes as "a big carnival of wannabes."

Pardon me, but a marathon isn't just a race. Rather it is a test of one's dedication, stamina, and endurance over many more grueling miles. Each long distance marathon runner strives to do his or her best. Not everyone is a gifted elite runner, and the marathon does not, and should not, belong only to "well-trained distance athletes," a.k.a. elites. In Boston, where there are age group qualifying times (which I qualified for seven times and ran five times with a non-chip PR of 3:57:03 at age nearly 56) rank amateurs are not kept home. Rather, they can train for and run with the Dana Farber Cancer Institute Team. They should not be labeled as lowly occasional joggers. They are athletes of all shapes, sizes, ages, and backgrounds wanting to achieve a dream, that of being a marathon finisher and earning that coveted finisher's medal. Speed is not always the foremost attribute. However, a combination of a runner's heart and soul, rather than a quest for money, propels one towards his or her goal, just as it does me.

At age 67, I am not the fast competitive runner I once was, yet completing marathons and competing against myself are still so special a challenge to me. I welcome the opportunity to test myself over and over and over again. Rank amateur? I think not! Often I am forced to dig deeper into my inner core of strength and determination to meet my goal. Is it a mortal sin for me to slow down at some point? Am I less of a marathon runner when I don't welcome "the wall" with joy and open arms? Only when you have overcome the effects of "hitting the wall" can you truly appreciate the effort and toll dealt by a 26.2 mile road race challenge. Is a senior running friend another classified "wannabe" in her quest to complete a marathon in all of our fifty states? I wonder how many younger elite athletes can lay claim to her daunting undertaking. I admire her tenacity and courage with these words: You go, girl!

Those of us fortunate enough to be able to run long distances have earned the right to be respected, not maligned, for our efforts and successes. How we get to a marathon starting line doesn't matter. That we reach the finish line does. To all labeled marathon "wannabes" and "rank amateurs" I offer these words of Langston Hughes: "Hold fast, hold fast your dreams; for if dreams die, life is a broken-winged bird that cannot fly."

Chapter Eleven - Catch the Racing Spirit

"Whoever wants to reach a certain goal must take many small steps" - *Helmut Schmidt, as quoted by James Markham in The New York Times*

The New Ed Erichson Run

After being held for many years at Dutchess Community College, the 1997 Ed Erichson Inaugural Run was held at a different location. Long heralded as the "wake up to spring" event, the race location had to be changed. It's best not to question why or why not, rather the focus should remain on the purpose of this event and the merits of a new location and different distances. This event honors a beloved runner, who tragically died at a young age, by donating money raised as a scholarship in his name to a chosen high school senior. Change can be quite a positive thing and runners excel at adapting.

It was with determination and anticipation that I signed up for the 10 miler. Last year breathing problems forced me to drop out of the 15K at the two mile mark, thereby losing my chance to tackle the challenging course. Now, as a runner, I needed to have redemption, completion, and a closure of sorts. A runner is often driven to run for many reasons and I was no exception.

A map of the new course hung in full view in the registration room; the five miler marked in red, the 10 miler marked in green. Anxiously I studied the map.

Hmmmm, one big long loop with a little "side arm" loop. Okay, so we are able to run the five mile route and a "bit extra." The "bit extra" did not look like another five miles in distance. My conclusion? The map must not be drawn to scale. Mentally I did what so many other runners do – I "ran" the course in my head, noting where turns would be, etc. Erroneously I also concluded that the course would be basically flat. I should have known better because nothing is really flat in that area.

However, it didn't take long for me to be shocked into reality. While Roy and I were planning a suitable spot to meet on the course, the truth came out from a volunteer that "it's a two loop course with a big, bad hill." What do you mean two loops? It looks like one big loop with an extra little loop. Wrong again!! My bubble had burst. Okay, I could handle two loops, just like I've done so many times for the Dutchess County Classic Marathon. But THE HILL twice, running AGAINST the wind? This definitely called for a different strategy. I had to shift gears and think hills and wind rather than nice flat stretches. The knots in my stomach became tighter . . .

The five mile racers preceded the 10 mile runners. I like less congestion at the start. Hey, I might even like the hills! The 10 mile race started with a bang and I immediately prepared to get into a comfortable warming-up running pace. Someone called out to me, "Erika, you're going out too fast." On the contrary, I was merely preparing to get into my own running groove. My leg turnover was comfortable. I continued doing it my way.

The road was basically level but open to some areas of crosswinds. Nothing looked familiar since I was running in the opposite direction to the marathon course. Still, the peaceful country setting was beautiful. Volunteers manned the crucial turning points. I felt like I was on a roll but not for long. You guessed it. It was hill running time. Going against the wind made this seemingly never ending upward trek feel like a grueling workout. Whew! Leg turnover was definitely slower and much more measured.

It was on this hilly section that I caught up with another runner who was going about my pace. We jokingly damned the wind, the hills, the sore legs, more wind, more hills, and more sore legs. The reward for conquering this long, uphill portion was a delightfully long downhill. We ran together for about another two miles before he pulled ahead. This was only his second 10 mile distance. I was impressed by his tenacity.

The hill on aptly named Croft Hill Road did not seem as foreboding the second time around. Perhaps this was due to the realization that it really was the last big obstacle before heading towards the finish line. A psychological boost for sure. I met Roy the second time around at about the eight mile mark and waved him off. No fluid replacements were needed. Soon I caught up to and passed the runner ahead of me, offering him verbal encouragement. My adrenaline seemed to reach an all-time high and, to my amazement, my legs really wanted to move!

The finish line was such a welcome sight. The clock showed 1:22:03 and, for me, the race was over. Not far behind was the runner who successfully completed his second 10 mile distance. He even won his age group award! Another runner made a grand approach as he got down on his hands and knees after crossing the finish line. A comical relief to any running stress.

The Ed Erichson Run has always been a great way to welcome the coming of spring and get one's running legs in shape. The new distance and course make this a "must" for me. The challenge of the hills is still there too.

For anyone who has done the earlier 15K distance, just know that the hills were not left behind in Poughkeepsie; they're awaiting you in LaGrange.

The 1998 Ed Erichson Memorial Races

I am a runner. I am also a runner with certain yearly desired races. One of these has been the Ed Erichson Runs, with the long race always appealing to my legs as a "wake up to spring" call.

Sometimes this is a rude awakening as it was for me with this year's 10 miler. I was ready, willing and able, sort of. My legs were not. In the end both of us were victorious albeit much slower than usual.

This year the Gods of Good Weather prevailed. Gone was the previous day's heavy snowfall - the roads were clear. In its place, cold, brisk winds echoed in the runners' footstrikes while temperatures hovered around 40 degrees. It was a near perfect day for runners. With a five miler billed as fast and flat and a challenging 10 miler, there was something for everyone.

For myself, I prefer distances of 15K or longer. Endurance suits me better than speed. I guess once I'm out there on the roads I like to stay there as long as possible. I also like these words by an unknown author: "Challenges - the harder the course the more rewarding the triumph."

I went for the double loop (and the double curse) - the upward climb at Croft Hill Road. Perhaps it was the nice downhill after the uphill pain that kept me going for more miles. Whatever it was, I think I had negative splits for the second loop.

The course is so familiar since part is run on the Dutchess County Classic Marathon route. It's strange how things look different in a marathon than from a 10 miler. The strong winds buffeted me. I felt like I was swaying to an unfamiliar melody. I recall waving to the course marshals, thanking them for being out there and telling them I'd lost my zip and probably was the last runner. Well, maybe it gave them a good laugh.

Well something had to happen since my legs did not have their usual bullet-like speed. Instead, they felt glued to the pavement. Not good. Runner after runner passed me. My legs still stayed glued to the pavement. A recent illness took more starch out of me than I thought. Oh, what the heck, I was having fun and glad to be racing again after a three month hiatus. I really felt like I held the whole world in my hands. Running can do that, you know.

A Successful First: The Firecracker 4K Race

Often I have trepidations when running a race held for the first time. Doubts are many and I wonder what "bugs" will befall the runners. Is it well organized? Is the course marked and marshaled? Will the results be scored correctly and in a timely manner? Is there water on the course? How will the timing device function? Is the course accurate? Are there restrooms? On and on I worry . . .

Well, I could have buried all my doubts about the first annual Firecracker 4K race in Kingston, New York in late June. Race personnel were most kind and courteous in answering my questions. As an early arrival (I was in unfamiliar territory and sure I would get lost so I allowed for ample driving time) I had many questions about the starting place, the course, locations of restrooms, etc. Even though the volunteers were busy setting up, everyone responded kindly to my inquiries.

I was amazed at how many participants showed up. They must have had faith in the event. Of course, my usual pre-race jitters prevailed. My spirits were buoyed by seeing so many runners whom I recognized. I felt like I was on home turf.

The race went off smoothly and as scheduled, which was a blessing because the heat and humidity were rapidly increasing. I liked the out and back course. It was flat, safe, and free of vehicular traffic. It's always a good feeling to know when you've reached the midway turnaround point. Running back seemed so much easier than going out. Distances were painted along the paved roadway, yet the final stretch back into Rotary Park seemed endless. A runner's anxiety can do that. In no time at all a competitor passed me. I recognized her beautiful long blonde hair and thought, "Oops, I'd better get movin'."

Race personnel, volunteers, and other runners gathered at the finish area when I arrived there. Their cheers were music to my ears. There was so much enthusiasm. Every participant probably felt as special as I did. I then joined them to cheer on other incoming runners and walkers.

Race results were timely tabulated and the trophies awarded were befitting of the occasion - a very patriotic red, white, and blue base. I considered myself fortunate to have won one. What a class act when a competitor came over and congratulated me. I had not met her before. I recall telling her that next year I'd be in a new age group. For now, however, I know who my competition is.

Running from the Heart

For runners it's easy. They just come and run with their hearts. It's that simple.

A case in point was the CHAIN Run, a five mile race recently held in Highland, New York. CHAIN stands for Community Helping Another In Need. The monies from this fundraising event were to help a young family overburdened with medical expenses for their two young children, both of whom suffer from a rare genetic disorder.

This particular event also featured a three mile race for walkers, which enabled more people to give from their hearts and participate. It was amazing to see how many participants lined up at the starting line. Doing something for someone in need far outweighed the desire to win an award. It was a tremendous outpouring of community spirit, with young and old alike recognizing that they can make a difference in the lives of others.

As an "older" runner I was in good company. Three of my running friends there that day are in their 50s, another is nearing the magical age of 70 and, of course, no race event would be complete without a certain spirited senior runner. At age 77 he's a human dynamo. What an inspiration!

The five mile course was a mixture of hills (you know, those LONG, never ending upward ones), some rolling bumps and grinds, and some level areas. There was a wonderful but deceptive downhill portion at the start. We breathed a sigh of relief, but not for long. Of course, what goes down must go up, and UP we did go! We traversed the rural areas of Highland, a real peaceful country setting. The next day's predicted snowstorm stalled long enough for the weather to cooperate, cold but sunny and bright. Ideal running conditions.

The most touching moments came during the awards ceremony when the race director introduced this special family. How lucky they are to see how special they are to this small community and to all who supported this event. A whopping $1900 was raised for this deserving family. May it show everyone in the county what the heart and soul of a community can do. This community may be small in size but it has a heart as big as all outdoors.

Runners don't really need prodding to come out and run. They just do it. That so many could come out in support of others in need shows that runners do have big hearts when it comes to giving.

The Viking 10K Remembered

Pain has its moments and memories . . .

The Viking 10K, held each year in late December, is a race that sounded challenging and "just up my alley." Recalling the words on the race application extolling the hills, I concluded that this race is really something I have to do. My legs are accustomed to hill running. Our town is blessed with many steep hills including the mighty Storm King Mountain traversed by two scenic roads. Hence my decision to run it was made. How bad could it be?

After a snowy start in 1994, the 1995 race day event presented the runners with cold but decent weather and roads that were clear enough to run on. I was still in the midst of battling suspected allergy-related breathing problems but decided to take the plunge . . . errrrr, the long upward trek. Despite an uncomfortable warm-up run, my enthusiasm to run it didn't diminish.

The race started and I could only run a quarter of a mile before breathing problems overtook me. I was no Viking! With tears streaming down my cheeks I had to drop out. This was such a blow to my spirit.

Because of this failed attempt, I was more determined than ever to return and conquer the hills in 1996. The weather wasn't cold and snowy this time; rather it was damp and raw with a heavy steady rainfall starting shortly before race time. It was as if the Viking Gods conspired once again to bring misery to the runners. I even overheard someone say something like, "C'mon rain, make it even more miserable." It was a mystery voice that came from out of nowhere.

The weather became more miserable the closer it got to the 1 PM starting time. No one was immune and we all looked like soggy, wet mops at the starting line. Complete with a Viking horn headpiece, the race director greeted this dauntless group of runners.

I ran past the quarter mile point of last year's drop-out site and tackled the first small hill with gusto. Well, perhaps it was only because the hill was short, not because I had so much vim, vigor and vitality. This spurt of gusto didn't last long.

The hills were relentless, always going upward, rarely level or with a nice downward slope. My legs were not too happy. They hurt and burned. My quads and calves were also painfully sore.

After the turnaround point I had to give in to the pain and power-walk a bit. My legs were rebelling at the prospect of tackling yet ANOTHER HILL. This is when another woman runner reached me. Instead of surging ahead she asked if I was okay and offered to run with me. She was willing to give up precious clock time to stay with me. Her gesture warmed my heart. However, I assured her that I was okay but that my legs were sore and rebelling against the punishment I was subjecting them to. God bless runners like her!

On the less serious side, I overheard a woman runner comment to her running partner about how glad that she was wearing (get ready for this!) WATERPROOF MASCARA! It was still raining heavily. I also was thankful that I was wearing the same thing. Otherwise, we both would have sported raccoon-like smudges around our eyes at the finish. This lighter moment made me chuckle. Forget about the hills. It was time to think about our mascara.

The rain continued throughout the race. Getting wetter was no longer a concern. It brought back to mind the words of the race director at the start, "It's raining now but it will be freezing rain on the way back." One must remember that the race application promised only miserable weather. I thought, "Isn't that the miserable truth!"

For some dumb reason I thought the way back would be easier and with more downhills. How wrong I was!!! Another runner's words about those hills being there all the time and worse on the way back were so true. If my abused legs were willing to forgive me earlier, they no longer would do so.

I kept sight of my guardian angel, a woman who ran with such an even, steady pace. I also flip-flopped places with another woman runner. She assured me that it would be all downhill once we'd reach the church. You can imagine how bug-eyed I was looking for a steeple in the distance.

It was a blessing for my legs when the final downhill appeared, followed by a level road that then led directly up to the finish line chutes. The freezing rain never materialized; just rain, rain, and more rain. Was it my imagination that this rain subsided shortly after the race ended?

Sometimes we runners just have to find humor in running a race like this. In its own punishing way this race provided just such a touch of humor. Afterwards I could laugh while recounting the challenge of the hills. It hurt too much to cry.

When asked which item I wanted for my age group award (choice of homemade apple pie, maple syrup, or honey), I was tempted to say, "one of each." I chose the magnificent jar of honey. It was a "sweet" ending to this day.

Given my options for future races, I'11 end this article with a quote from General Douglas MacArthur: "I shall return."

A Runner's View of the 2004 Orange Classic

"The one who has no imagination, has no wings." - Author Unknown

What started as a vision became a reality in mid-June when the Orange Classic 10K reverted to a Sunday race date and offered a new more rural course. It was then that Roy and I decided to run our first Orange Classic race. Preferring more rural routes, the new course appealed to us. It was also our way of saying "thank you" to the race director for all that he has done for and given to the running community. We had to lend our support to his imagination and future dreams for this event.

The Gods of Good Weather shined brightly on the runners at the start. What a thrill to be there! Roy's bib number was 76 and I likened him to the "Spirit of '76." Fresh off an eight mile uphill footrace at Whiteface Mountain, we decided to cast aside racing heroics and have fun as we ran. My tired legs did a lot of walking and I even stopped to pick up coins along the roadside. Having fun was more a part of the equation for me than actually racing hard on legs that did not welcome any more inclines. I thanked the many volunteers and police personnel and enjoyed the music and spectators' cheers. The many participants supporting this event is a testimony to the spirit within the running community.

Bill Rodgers handed out age group awards and another runner and I had our bib numbers autographed by him. What a gracious and unassuming person. He told me that his daughter's name is Erika, spelled with a "k" like mine. I told him about my twin sister, Heidi, and I being named after heather that grew side by side in Germany.

After the race I heard some remarks about the course having too much concrete, being too "industrial," and questioning why it was held at a mall. For me, I liked the course, the trees, the serenity I found, and the chance to run on an untested route. I recalled these words:

"For life to be meaningful you must have a challenge."
- Author Unknown

Chapter Twelve - High Anxiety

"Life is either a daring adventure or nothing." – Helen Keller

Running On Empty - A Human Race Experience

It was one of those mornings. You know the kind - you're preregistered for a race but aren't really "geared up to go." It's a dreary day, hazy, raining, and much too humid. The saturated air hangs low like a thick unwanted cloud. You really aren't inclined to move your legs, much less run a race. Those were my feelings on Labor Day when I had to force myself to get up for the long drive to the site for a new race – The Human Race 5K Race of Champions. Allergy problems abounded and an unsettled stomach would not quiet down. Needless to say, I did not even feel like I was part of the human race!

This 5K event benefitted a worthwhile organization. It just didn't seem right not to show up.

Activity was in full swing when I arrived at the check-in table. I disliked the humidity but I welcomed the cool, refreshing drizzle. Everyone seemed so helpful and pleasant. Late runners from the earlier four mile race were enthusiastically being greeted in and the finish line was a hub of congratulatory activity. I did a short warm-up run and knew I would be running on empty - all my energy would have to go to combating my allergies. The humid air seems to trap all the airborne allergens and my breathing gets labored. It's not medically unsafe, just downright uncomfortable and not conducive to fast race times. Had it not been for my husband's encouragement and confidence (he is the "wind beneath my wings") I probably would have dropped out of the race completely.

Anyhow, I gave it my all and completed the race. The finish line was such a welcomed sight that I didn't even glance at the clock. I may have been running on empty during the race but afterwards my cup sure did runneth over. I was shocked to learn that I had an award-winning time (22:14, 1st Masters). Most of all, I felt I had completed the race, albeit laboriously, for a great cause. This, more than anything else, made me feel good about myself and in being part of this special event.

When the Going Gets Tough, and the Tough Can't Get Going

We all know the saying "When the going gets tough, the tough get going." Well, I am one "tough cookie" who couldn't get going.

The year began with promises of more good competitive running. However, this was short-lived. With one race into the New Year behind me, my running came to an abrupt end one January day with a painful foot injury. Down and out time!

After too many weeks of not being able to run, my sanity was tested to the limit. It was not until early March that I could resume pounding the pavement, albeit lightly. Although trepidations were many, I successfully completed the Boston Marathon in April, thinking that this was the start of more good running times. This elation also was short-lived.

The cold, snowy days of winter were replaced with budding days of spring. A pattern soon developed as these new growths of spring came into being. Pollen reigned supreme while my running took a nose dive. My allergies were really hit hard; the worst I'd ever experienced.

In races I just "didn't have it." After a mile or two breathing became labored and uncomfortable and my legs felt sluggish. It was tough going.

Training runs were no better. Wheezing replaced rhythmic breathing. Previously easy hills became formidable mountains. My chest felt sore after each run. Every race became a battle between me and nature's elements. Nature claimed the victory.

The more that I tried to run, the worse I felt. The worse I felt, the more depressed I became. I was stymied. Runners HAVE to run. These battles with Mother Nature took their toll. It became an all-out war against allergies.

The truth of the matter was that I couldn't go on this way. Race times were off while breathing problems were on the rise. I know that I am tough, but this was ridiculous.

In desperation I turned to an allergy specialist to help me with these tough times. While currently undergoing allergy and medical tests, I am still plodding along trying to get back the zip that was zapped.

One consolation is that I can always THINK SNOW!! When running times are really hard, I shift gears and think about the pollen-free days of winter, the refreshing cool, crisp air that abounds, and the cushioning feeling of a snowfall.

I suspect that my competitive spirit won't be on hold for too long a time. "Tough times don't last, but tough people do!"

The DNF Zone

DNF stands for DID NOT FINISH. It's what I've had to mark in my running log next to too many races in which I couldn't reach the finish line. Knowing that you've had a DNF race doesn't increase your confidence in your running or racing ability. It certainly knocked mine down the drain.

DNFs made 1994 the summer of my discontent. Actually, my DNF Zone extended far beyond the summer. Just when I thought I'd gotten into my winter comfort zone another DNF greeted me. It was disheartening to yearn to run or race only to have to give in to breathing problems and drop out.

Overcoming ever-increasing DNFs was accomplished by stopping all competitive running and impatiently waiting for the grass pollen to die down and go away. In October I started an immunotherapy program of weekly injections of grass pollen to eventually build up my immune system. Oh how much I longed to get back on a roll with running! The cold, crisp air of winter is my forte and I thrive like a polar bear . . . usually.

In December I jubilantly returned to Central Park after a six month hiatus from racing there. My spirits were buoyed by the colder temperatures. Successfully running earlier races of ten miles and 25K put me on a runner's high. The exhilaration of speed was in my blood and I soared like an eagle . . . but not for long.

The early predicted cold, snowy days just didn't occur in January. Yet I somehow found myself at the starting line of another ten miler in Central Park. The hills were mine for the taking and I was ready! It was unseasonably humid and the thick air enveloped me with an unwanted moist blanket. With temperatures reaching the high 50s, I felt smothered. Everything around me seemed to have a greenish hue. I thought, "hold the pollen, it's not springtime yet."

My immune system had not yet started to respond to the weekly immunotherapy injections. Consequently, it didn't take long for these injections to bring about my downfall. I had met my Waterloo. An allergic reaction of considerable magnitude produced symptoms of shortness of breath. I could not run beyond a mile or so. It was time to drop out . . . time for another DNF Zone of Disappointment.

Runners may remember seeing me at the second Winter Series 5K race – I was forlornly walking in the opposite direction. Shortness of breath forced me to drop out after about a quarter of a mile. It was another DNF to log in for '95.

My heart and mind know that, with my allergy problems, things might get worse before they get better. It will take a while for me to build up an immune response. The possibility of some kind of allergic reaction following the injections is always present. I have a long way to go with the treatment program.

Still, I yearn to race. As always, my inborn competitive spirit doesn't go away. Running is too much a part of my life. I do not like occupying the DNF Zone.

Help! Get me outta here!

When the Heat is On

The weatherman predicted another 3-H day: hazy, hot, and humid. He lied. Oh, how he lied! It was a 4-H day: hazy, hot, humid, and HORRIBLE. You know, one of those days where lazily lying on a sandy beach and taking in a minimum of sun and a maximum of soothing ocean swimming is paramount to any thoughts of running on the sizzling hot pavement.

You're a maxed-out runner, beaten to the pulp by the heat and drenched equally as much from the humidity as from moving your feet in a forward direction. Today the only steps you've taken have been to and from the shoreline. You are wearing rubberized flip-flop sandals instead of running shoes. You do not propel your feet in the fast forward mode. Another day perhaps . . . Today it's cruising over the sand in slow motion. Very slow motion . . .

Your feet feel temporarily soothed and your thoughts run back to the past. You recall another time on this same beach where, in the coolness of the previous autumn temperatures, you ran along the soft, sandy shoreline enjoying the outgoing tide, the cool ocean breezes, and the warming effects of the rising sun at daybreak.

With the once-populated beach being devoid of humans, only low flying seagulls are there to keep you company. The warm water of summer is much colder now as it lathers the sand. The tide begins to shift, something you didn't realize earlier. As you run you leave footprints in the wet sand of a quickly vanishing shoreline. Out and back goes the tide, exposing less and less of the sandy beach. Seashells glisten in the slowly rising sun. It's a perfect morning for running.

At the end of this sandy expanse is a rocky formation. You recall making a decision to boldly traverse this obstacle. You call it your mini Escarpment Trail run.

Another time you remember running this same route during a ferocious rainstorm. This time the low flying objects are not seagulls but twigs, driftwood, and anything else not tied down that the wind can toss around like a misguided missile.

The darkened sky is filled with menacing clouds swiftly moving across the horizon. The tide is rushing in with a fury, whipping at your ankles as it hits the shoreline. How hard it is to buck the relentless headwind! Yet, as you run, you feel strangely at peace in this unsettled atmosphere. Running does that to you.

A runner can't change the weather but the weather can alter the plans of a runner. All that the runner has to do is go out and keep on truckin' or give in to the whims of nature. The latter means missing out on another challenge and losing another chance to run. The former means going for that special kind of exhilaration that only running can give.

When the heat is on adjust your running schedule accordingly. Don't be beaten by the heat. All other times get out there and, as the Nike motto states, "just do it!"

When Your Zip, Zest, and Zeal Have Been Zapped

This article is geared toward those runners who yearn for the quick return of the hot weather and the hasty exit of Old Man Winter.

The outside temperature rises to the near 100 degree mark while the equally high humidity hovers all around creating a sauna-like effect. It's another hazy, hot, and humid afternoon. It's a real "dog day of summer."

The runner starts her run slowly, toting a full bottle of water, and wipes the rapidly accumulating wetness from her brow. It increases with each footstrike and arm swing. It clings to her skin like saran wrap. Some of the sweat drips on her cheeks like glistening raindrops. The taste of salt touches her lips. A sweep of the hand brings only temporary relief. About a mile down the road the intense heat and sun create a mirage. No matter how hard she tries, the runner can't reach the imaginary spot of water. Her eyes are playing cruel tricks. Thank God for the trusty water bottle she carries.

The bright sun continues to shine relentlessly with glee as it directs its seething rays downward. The pavement is hot. Searing heat shoots up the runner's feet and legs resulting in sluggish legs and ever so slow footstrikes. The rhythmic flow of her arms is reduced to a slow limp swing, barely able to propel her along. It's HOT!!

The runner's pace picks up a bit on the shady downhill as the sun plays hide and seek with the trees - an all too brief respite. The trees trade places with the open road again. The sun seems to be wearing a smirky smile. The shaded areas become few and far between. More mirages appear.

It's a long, hard seven mile run. Too ambitious an undertaking for a hot summer day. With about one mile to go there are two more uphills to tackle. The once full water bottle is empty. The mirages continue. Talk about dropping in one's tracks.

On the final uphill portion a neighbor comes to the rescue, refilling the empty bottle with soothing fresh water spiked with lemon slices. A million bucks couldn't repay this kindness.

What the runner thought was going to be an enjoyable run turned out to be a tedious effort to put one foot in front of the other. It was much hotter than expected. She was not prepared for the sun's savage attack. It was a lesson learned the hard way.

I prefer to bid adieu to these sauna days. Bring on the snow and the cool, crisp wintry air. Let winter stay forever.

To Run or Not to Run

It was the kind of day that lended itself to make good excuses for not running. This was the fourth day in a row with July's temperatures coming in April and where spring was bypassed by the emergence of summer's dreaded soaring temperatures and humidity. Another day starting out so hot and humid that one could envision steam coming from the pavement. To run or not to run?

As often noted, I am not a hot weather person. Twelve months of winter would suit me just fine. Three straight days of running (well, putting one slow foot in front of the other is a more accurate description of my pace) sapped my energy. I was wilted. Enough already! Parts of my body not previously exposed to the sun took on a reddened color. The sun's rays were not too kind even before a pre 9 AM start. Therefore, on day four, I vacillated and procrastinated for quite a while.

My running routes varied. One time it was about eight miles up to High Point on Route 218 in the Hudson Valley and back. A nighttime heavy rainfall had forced the road's closure. How wonderful to have the road all to myself! Being that I was higher up and next to the Hudson River a nice breeze helped cool me down a bit. Dripping beads of sweat turned to salt crystals. I took in the magnificent view of the Hudson Highlands, the Newburgh-Beacon Bridge, and Bannerman's Island. Nothing seemed to be moving except a train on the opposite side of the river. A stream of water cascaded down the mountain going into a culvert near the road. It looked so refreshingly cool. This is good I thought.

For my runs the following two days I shortened my distance to between five and six miles. The sun's rays beat down unmercifully and were made worse by the higher humidity. Talk about sluggish legs carrying on their own battle! Still I slowly plodded onward.

How verdant my surroundings were. Flowers presented a palette of colors and were nature's gift to the eyes. I marveled at how quickly all the buds opened. There was no way to avoid the direct sunlight as my routes always took me up a hill directly into the sun's path. My eyes squinted from its brightness and my own dripping perspiration. I was not a happy camper. One day a quick stop at a local hospital gave me a chance to replenish my nearly empty water bottle. A brief respite. Oh the wonderful cooling effect of air conditioning however short-lived it was! On the road again a frisky baby rabbit brought a smile to my face. I wished I had such energy.

On the fourth day higher humidity and slightly lower temperatures were predicted. Did I want to look like I had been caught in a downpour again? Did I really want to face the debilitating elements of nature? Of course! So out I went, starting with a slow gait and gradually evening out my pace. I saw a squirrel trying to outrun me start to cross the street. Half way across, my heavy footstrikes scared him and he quickly scurried away. It was pleasantly a bit less humid and not yet quite as hot. A gentle wind cooled me and I actually picked up the pace. A dog's barking greeted me at the top of the steep back road hill. It should know me by now as I have gone past this house so often on my runs. Its owner greeted me with a hearty "Hi."

Over these four days I found a total of 46¢ in loose change. I met a rabbit, a squirrel and a dog. I smelled the flowers and admired the beauty of the daffodils, tulips and hyacinths that abounded. I waved to the local barber in town. I laughed. So much positiveness from such negative weather.

To run or not to run? I decided to tackle the elements and came out ahead. I am glad I made the decision to look beyond the discomfort of the heat and humidity. I am glad I chose to run.

A Running Story with a Twist

If it had occurred during the days of Chubby Checker I could lay legitimate claim to performing one heck of a twist maneuver. Alas, a twisted left ankle was the only ungraceful movement I made. Not even an Oscar-winning performance.

Having taken enough days off from running due to right foot heel and arch pain, I was so thrilled to be back on the roads again The words to the song "Oh What a Beautiful Morning" tugged at my heartstrings. Just imagine how the elation of running put me in seventh heaven and on cloud nine. Then it happened.

One moment I was running, the next I was in a crumpled heap on the frozen ground. My left leg gave out. It just went numb. I landed hard. Fortunately, I didn't hear anything go snap, crackle, or pop (one has to look for humor at a time like this). However, a twisted left ankle and a badly scraped knee resulted.

I hugged a nearby sign post with all of my might for support. Once the ankle discomfort subsided for weight-bearing, I tried walking, then running. This painful interruption made me so angry that I was determined to finish my planned run. In hindsight, that probably wasn't the smartest thing to do. Me, stubborn? Never. Persistent? Always. I am my father's daughter to the nth degree.

After a while my left shoe felt very tight and I made a mental note to loosen its laces as soon as I got back into town. When I finally stopped, there was an oversized goose egg where my ankle once was and a large bloody hole in the knee area of my running tights. Not good. Once home, the injured ankle and foot resembled a palette of unsightly colors. The knee quickly stiffened and my whole body ached from the impact. I may roll well with the punches, but I am not a graceful twister.

With no evidence of broken ones or stress fractures, my doctor negated running but allowed me to walk and tended to my sore heel. Even with this, I feared that my sunny disposition would still take a downward spiral. A few walking breaks into town and to the library helped my psyche. For a while I heeded my inner sane voice and resisted the temptation to run. Probably most runners have faced a similar dilemma where walking just did not suffice.

After ten very restless days, the open roads beckoned and the runner in me took charge. Under Roy's watchful eye and in the midst of a snowstorm, a 3.7 mile run was done. The snow provided a soothing, cushioning effect. Roy had the assurance that a compulsive wife would not overdo it. And I didn't . . . this time!

Two weeks after my fall I had to test the limits of my healing, dissuade fears of another sudden fall, and take to the open roads on my own. Fear can be a powerful hindrance, which I hoped to balance with a determined heart and soul. In reality, I needed to run again. It was upsetting to Roy that I covered 8.1 miles without telling him what I might do that day. I may have given him a few more gray hairs and worry lines. Yet, my grin was larger than that of the Cheshire Cat.

The irony is that things got worse a short time later and life for me became "de agony of de feet." Being grounded was my ultimate fate. My sanity was tested . . . and still is.

Bridging the Gap

It was a crisp, cool fall morning. The kind that readily entices one to get out and run. So it was for Roy and me. Spurring us on was the recent opening of the Newburgh-Beacon ferry. It was Roy's idea to drive to the port in Newburgh, ride the ferry across the Hudson River to Beacon's train station, then run back to the starting port by traversing the Newburgh-Beacon Bridge. Give me an idea and I'll run with it. This is how I felt as we started our journey, hoping that my fear of heights would not negatively impact Roy's bright idea.

With this in mind, I recalled a recent hike to the fire tower atop Stissing Mountain in Pine Plains that my twin sister talked me into doing. Hiking to the base was no problem. Reaching the top of the tower was. I froze in my tracks on my upward trek with a mere three flights of stairs left, leaving my twin sister concerned that she might have to carry me down to terra firma. After regaining my equilibrium I went down one flight sitting on my backside, then turned around, grabbed the side railings and slowly inched my way down each remaining step. Therefore, I knew that if I got out of my comfort zone on the bridge's span and froze like a zombie, Roy might have to carry me the rest of the way across.

Our run, about a 10K in total distance, started with a long uphill climb to the east side of the bridge. We tried to follow the painted road arrows of the 5-Mile Bridge Run in reverse. We had never traversed the bridge by running across it. The metal plates rattled under our feet. Traffic whizzed by. A cool wind wrapped us in its grasp. The water below widened. I hugged the side closest to the roadway and felt like I was holding on for dear life while Roy stayed right behind me. Once committed, there was no way to go but forward. My courage was at an all-time low. I froze in my tracks at mid-span, with dizziness overtaking me. I tried not to look down at the water. The memory of the fire tower's height came back to haunt me. Slowly, with Roy's steady encouragement, I put one shaky foot in front of the other until I could move more fluidly. More than an hour after we started out adventurous run, we reached the parking lot and watched the ferry make its last morning crossing back to the port. It, too, had finished its early morning run schedule.

Our next run will be done in reverse, starting at the Newburgh end, running eastward across the span, and ending at the Beacon train station where we'll take the ferry back to port. I am, however, considering wearing blinders across the bridge. With tunnel vision and following the straight and narrow, this may be my savior when my courage is left by the roadside.

When Up is Down - A Triathlon with a Twist

BACKGROUND: Roy and his friend Tom preregistered as a Two Man Team in the Lake Dunmore Triathlon held in late July. Early race packet pick up time was Saturday July 28th between 9 AM and 5 PM.

REALITY: You know it's going to be a bad day when... Late Friday night Tom's enthusiasm took a nosedive when he fell and injured his ankle - actually HE took the nosedive! Our Saturday 7 AM meeting start lagged and we didn't hit the road until nearly 9:50 AM knowing that our destination was not a mere hop, skip, and jump away. Barbara, Tom's girlfriend, baptized her sweatshirt with an early morning cup of coffee. Tom's rear car tire picked up a huge nail and soon had that deflated look. Following Roy's directions, we reached a dead end street with Lake Champlain at our feet, the ferry on the OTHER side and the time already rapidly inching past 4 PM. Dark clouds loomed in the distance, heralding the presence of a threatening thunderstorm that waited to greet us. A frantic search for the Town Green in Middlebury ended as a lesson in futility.

Despite these trials and tribulations, we reached our destination at 5:06 PM, relieved that the place was still open for packet pickup. Tom concluded that he would be able to do the run, albeit a bit slower, so the team of Tom and Roy planned and prepared to conquer Lake Dunmore. Barbara and I looked forward to relaxing while the men did all the work! So we ate, drank, and were merry. Vermont and all its amenities were ours to enjoy.

At breakfast the next morning, Tom calmly asked me how I felt. I sheepishly replied, "All things considered, pretty good," already planning my lazy day in the sun while supporting the guys in their soon-to-be Herculean efforts. Or so I thought! With that Tom announced that his ankle was swollen and exhibited a multitude of colors. Clearly he could not do the running segment. I would have to sub for him. Since there were no three person teams allowed, Barbara was also "called into action" to do the canoe part with Tom. The Two Man Team suddenly transformed into a Four Person Mixed Team. "US? No, guys, you don't really mean US, do you?" Having only canoed a maximum of four miles in three previous outings, Barbara unexpectedly received her initiation into the world of competitive sports.

The 9.3 mile long run was certainly a rude awakening and my legs vehemently protested the trail running part. I must have uttered a multitude of ouches, among other more silent words. Getting off to a good start after I survived the run, Roy performed well on the thirty-seven mile bike route and relieving me of further agony on the course. Barbara survived her first ever competitive sports event by successfully canoeing the seven mile lake course with Tom. Our up-to-down day definitely ended on an upswing. We will all remember Lake Dunmore as the triathlon with a twist.

The Morning Casts a Dark Shadow

It's 5:00 AM. The air is unmoving and the humidity hangs suspended like a heavy unwanted blanket. It is dark, with the morning sun just starting to rise from its sleepy nest. Specks of gray clouds decorate the darkened sky. The intense heat from the previous day's sun still lingers in the air.

An early morning runner heads for the unblemished school track, pausing to run through the misty grass and to smell the freshness of a new day . . . and to enjoy the unbroken silence. In the distance an eerie, darkened shadow looms, slowly moving on the track, neither running nor walking, but shuffling along like a displaced gargoyle or a resurrected Quasimodo, often hidden by the dark branches of nearby trees or the wooden spectators' viewing stands.

The lone runner approaches the track, eager to catch a first glimpse of the newly-born sunrise soon to appear on the horizon, to relish the peaceful solitude and to embrace yet another day of life. Already the humidity forms beads of sweat with each succeeding step. Soon the blackened shadow comes into view. The runner pauses, then passes, while the darkened figure is silent with watchful eyes.

The two meet again as the runner completes the second lap. No words are spoken, but the unknown figure breathes heavily and makes panting sounds as the runner passes. His garments are so incongruous for a hot, humid morning – long, heavy sweatpants, outer windbreaker jacket, and a dark woolen cap. A man strangely attired for an early morning run, certainly not a typical runner.

Not to be intimidated by the "intruder," the runner continues another lap around the track, each step bringing with it a rapidly mounting fear. Her mind tells her to leave but her feet feel glued to the pavement. The figure's panting and heavy breathing escalate to louder grunting animal-like sounds.

As the growling and grunting continue to permeate the stillness, the runner, fueled with a spurt of adrenaline and almost too late wisdom prepares to run for all she is worth. At the same time, another regular morning runner arrives and strides quickly to the track. She recognizes him. She is safe!

Within a few minutes the now mute stranger disappears into the parking lot. A car's engine starts. The dark shadows give way to the bright, rising sun.

A follow-up message: I treasured my early morning runs and when a stranger appeared on the track I did not want to be forced or intimidated to leave. Unwisely, I stayed there, even though it was a fearful situation. Had the other regular runner not appeared, I could have experienced unpleasant or dangerous consequences.

When I noticed an unfamiliar car in the parking lot, I should have exercised caution before venturing out alone onto the darkened track. It would have been wise to quickly jot down its license plate number beforehand. Knowing that the stranger was not a regular runner, I NEVER should have stayed. The woolen cap could have been pulled over his face, affording him a perfect disguise. The potentials for danger were immeasurable.

Fortunately nothing happened that morning, but for many weeks that followed I was scared every morning when I approached that area. Carefully and cautiously I surveyed the parking lot for unfamiliar cars and scrutinized the track for any shadows. At that point, my own shadow would have frightened me!

I learned a valuable lesson. How much better it is to run for fun than have to run in fear of one's life. "Running scared" is not my idea of quality running.

The Ghost Train

By the time I arrived at Rockland Lake for my usual after-work run, the weather had taken a BIG turn for the worse. Dark, threatening skies blocked out any bit of remaining daylight and wind gusts discriminately blew the sleet, freezing rain, and snow mixture. I listened to my heart, not my mind, and decided to "go for it." No sooner had I reached the Nature Center, a mere fraction of a mile out, when I was brought to a dead stop. The fierce wind met me head-on, beating me with sharp, cold pellets of ice. For a few stunned moments I stood there, deciding whether or not to try or cry, turn around and go back, or forge ahead with all my might. I did two out of three, pretending to be a pioneer crossing the Donner Pass in the High Sierras of California. Running forward was nearly impossible. As long as I kept my head down I could avoid some direct hits to my face. The wind was as persistent in its efforts to blow me into the water as I was determined to stay on the beaten path.

After doggedly running about a mile or so, I noticed the velocity of the wind. Tree tops seemed to dip lower and lower. I listened for crackling sounds, thinking any moment now a tree branch would snap off. All the barren tree limbs looked like they wanted to snatch me up as they swayed against a backdrop of eerie gray skies. Then I heard it! A train was coming!!! It was bearing down on where I was running! I felt fear, then panic. A childhood memory of many years earlier flashed by. Then, I was crossing railroad tracks when I spotted a large locomotive coming at me. It missed me by inches as I jumped off into a side gully. Then reality again set in. Soon the noise quieted down and I realized I had already run to the south parking lot. My ghost train was nowhere in sight . . . or so I thought.

The icy pavement crunched under my feet as I ran to the turnaround point at the firehouse. There, six deer greeted me and I could almost touch them when three of them ventured across the road directly in front of me. These regal-looking deer were a delight to see when all else around me was gloomy, cold and unfriendly. The temperature dropped rapidly and my planned seven mile run would now become a six mile run. I disregarded all plans to retrace my steps along the inner path around the lake. Ghost or not, I did not want to think about another train coming from out of nowhere. The pelting of ice on my face continued, no matter which way I turned to run. The final one mile straightaway road awaited me. Then it came, that horrible sound - the ghost train was on the straightaway!! Louder and louder the wind howled. Closer and closer the sound of an approaching locomotive came. Oh no, my feet are wet and frozen. I can't run fast any more . . .

Afterwards I thought about how many tricks nature's sounds can play on us. My ghost train was not real, yet it certainly sounded real and threatening. The sound actually came from several swans flapping their wings while landing on the water. Perhaps I'll stay indoors next time. On second thought, NO WAY! I'm too adventurous.

The Heart of a Runner

"Some of us think holding on makes us strong, but sometimes it is letting go." These words gave me the idea for this article. You see, I must learn to let go of a sport I have done for 24 years, one-third of my life. As of now, it's a fate worse than death. No more time for heroics as the die has been cast. Slowly I must deal with my psyche and accept this probable reality. The abruptness of it all still has not set in. The heart of a runner just can't stop beating.

Years of hard pavement pounding and long distance running caused major damage to my right knee. I suspect the same holds true for the left knee. The downward spiral began in late February 2010 when, while walking during a heavy snowstorm, I failed to leap over a large snow mound. The knee emitted an audible crunch. Navigational skills were obviously not my forte. Pain and physical therapy sessions became the norm as I longed to tackle the open roads, only to face another calamity. During a 5K race in late May, I lost my footing on a banked curb and hit the cruelly unforgiving hard sidewalk with a loud thump with my bad knee. Murphy's Law reigned supreme.

Weeks passed, and facial road rash and related injuries healed, my purple-tinted leg and foot returned to an almost normal color, and I hoped to resume running and racing with my usual gusto. Alas, this was not to be. Forget running – it was all I could do to even walk my beloved short running routes. The doctor kept telling me that my running days were over as two MRI scans confirmed our worst fears. Oh how I resisted listening to his words – "No more running, Erika."

So, this past October I underwent arthroscopic knee surgery to repair the damaged knee, being ever so optimistic it would be a cure-all for my pain. While a meniscus tear was repaired and a knee bone scraping was done, the softness of my bone did not make me a candidate for surgical drilling needed to stimulate bone growth. Another down day.

In the days that followed I hobbled and tried to resume walking, all the while yearning for what was and fearing what would be. This runner's heart was skipping too many beats. Perhaps I should count my many blessings enjoying what I can do while not focusing on what I cannot. Perhaps I can become as successful as a walker as I did as a runner.

Thus, life for me as a runner may be winding down as I hesitantly tackle the roads ahead with a different passion and stride. I may not be able to turn back the clock, but I can rewind it to a different tick. Yes, one day I will smile broadly again and even perhaps try slow running. This runner's heart may beat to a different rhythm after all. In the final analysis, you can break the body but not the spirit.

Chapter Thirteen - Reflections

"Life is like an ice cream cone - you have to lick it." – Author Unknown

"Success is not about spontaneous combustion. You must set yourself on fire." – Maleah Davis

The Need to Run

When I initially took those first running steps it was done on a dare from a younger co-worker. I did not need to lose weight, meet people, or enter competitive events. In short, I didn't even think I needed to run. How much that has changed since 1986.

Through continued running I learned to like myself and rediscovered my artistic and athletic talents. I learned about the "inner me" and to appreciate all the positives I had in life. Problems became less magnified as running took hold of my heart and my life.

How free I felt when I ran. How good it felt to be in control of where I directed my footstrikes. How beautiful life and my surroundings had become. Running reintroduced me to the joys of laughter, strange as it may seem, and introduced me to my husband Roy.

While my initial running distance barely measured an out-of-breath mile, I went on to run marathons, ultras, and even complete the Big Apple Triathlon in 1988.

Running brought a whole new world to my doorstep. I became energized and challenged. I became alive!

I had found my niche through running. I had found a place of peace and freedom. Problems were easier to tackle. I embraced the running community with open arms. I smiled more and made many new friends. My artistic talents were reborn and I enjoyed drawing and sketching again. Creative writing also became a relaxing hobby. I was not afraid to risk criticism because I did not have to be perfect. I just had to run and let everything else fall into place.

Do I need to run? Absolutely yes! Running keeps the "new me" alive and well. Running challenges me. Running, in a sense, defines the whole person that I am. Running brings out all the aspects of my being and allows me to be free to be me.

I really need to run.

Catching the Running Spirit

Reflections energize the mind, body, soul and spirit. So it is with this in mind as I reflect back on my life as a late-in-life runner.

This is how I started. My only early experience running came as an eighth grade relay team runner. I was fast but my twin sister was faster. Our four-person team won the relay. End of story.

Fast forward many decades later. While living in Binghamton, New York in the early 1980s, I occasionally ran a bit with my youngest son, a fashion buff of a teenager. With limited financial resources, I wore whatever athletic attire I could choose from. He often said that he was so embarrassed to be seen running with me because my outfits were not stylish. Then, on Easter Sunday 1985, I mentioned to my middle son that I would someday like to run the New York City Marathon. Without missing a beat he said, "Go for it, Mom!" Thus, this future long distance runner finally embarked on really running seriously on April 1, 1986.

Seventeen months later, I ran my first New York City Marathon in 4:48:59, taking nearly 20 long minutes to reach the starting line. No chips then. As previously described, my outfit consisted of bright pink terry cloth shorts, the only pair I had, and a matching light pink T-shirt. A co-worker had earlier nicknamed me "Wonder Weed." With this in mind, I had ERIKA printed on the front and WONDER WEED printed on the back. Try explaining that one while traversing the streets of New York! Unknown to me, my co-workers bet money on how many miles I would run. When I finished the entire 26.2 miles, I got enough cash to buy a new pair of running shoes. I was elated.

Running became my passion. Guys noticed me. I smiled often. I was featured several times in the local newspaper. I had fame but no fortune. A friend at work gave me the perfect birthday gift – a real runner's outfit. Now I could dress like a true athlete. How cool was that?

These are some "how silly of me" reflections. It was at my first ever race, a local 5K. Oh, how I took such care to remove my T-shirt and pin on my bib number as perfectly centered as possible! The only problem was that I pinned it onto the back of the T-shirt and then felt so foolish when another runner tactlessly told me that bib numbers go on the front. This embarrassed me so much that I let my feet do the redemption, clocking 26:08 to place fifth (40-49). Another time I had to beat the darkness to get in my planned run after work. My Lycra tights felt "funny," being tight on the front of my knees, and bulging at the back. Yep! My tights were on backwards. I once ran 40 laps on the track to get in my 10 miles, all in the pouring rain. My outfit was not waterproof and weighed heavily on my shoulders. I felt like a wrinkled Quasimodo when I finally finished.

I recall racing a 5K a mere 13 days after a nasty bike fall. Following facial plastic surgery, along with my broken shoulder in a sling and "flying high" on codeine medication, I propelled my way to a 2nd 50-59 place in 23:43. Would a positive drug test result have banned me for life?

Personal bests were many and my three sons were in awe of what their ever-lovin' mother could do. Goals were made and met. Long distances became my passion. In all, I've completed 39 marathons and 11 ultras, including a 60K in 6:22:41 and a 50K PR in 4:53:21. My PR for a marathon is 3:37:17 at the 1993 Dutchess County Classic Marathon. These were all non-chip times. My best Boston is 3:57:03 (no chip) in 1994 and my best New York City Marathon is 3:56:46 (no chip) in 1992. Memorable "Only One Hill" races are one completed Mt. Washington Run Up and four Whiteface Mountain uphill treks. Oh, the aching quads!

I credit my running ability to my parents. My Mom could out-walk anyone except her own mother (my grandmother). My Dad aspired to run in the 1936 Berlin Olympics, a dream he never realized or forgot. He instilled in my three sisters and me the love of walking among nature's terrain and creatures. It was a Sunday ritual in my youth. It seems I have been putting one foot in front of the other for a long, long time. That it evolved into running later on in my life is no surprise to me.

Now, 24 years later, when I look back in time and reflect on my long running career, I do so with great pride, immense joy, and a wonderful sense of accomplishment. How special is that?

Running for Someone

Did you ever run for someone? I don't mean actually running in place of another runner, but running for someone who you wanted to take along in your thoughts. A special friend, spouse, family member, someone from your past or present who touched your life in a memorable way, a cancer or AIDS victim? Or it may have been someone you happened to think about at a particular moment in time.

Often before starting out on my solo runs Roy will say, "Run a mile for me, hon." I'll say "No way! A mile isn't enough. I'll run them ALL for you."

Usually I run for the enjoyment of just being out there somewhere, doing my thing, thinking my thoughts, counting my blessings, disliking my job and the hassles it creates, and somehow feeling wonderfully free with each footstrike. This is my time to run for me and to take someone along in my thoughts while my feet rhythmically hit the pavement.

Then one day I did just what I am writing about. I ran one for George. As I ran I said aloud "Hey, George, this run is for you."

Who's George you ask, and why was I running for him, you wonder?

Well, George was a fellow older runner and consummate athlete, someone unknown to probably most of the local running community. Yet he could easily have represented someone you all know or may have met at one time or another.

George supported running. He was affectionately known to many of us as "The Guru." Yet his warm, friendly manner and enthusiasm for running welcomed runners beyond the county boundary. His wit and wisdom were spread far and wide, in marathons across the United States and on the streets of New York City where he worked as a policeman for many years.

If George wasn't running a marathon, he was there for fellow participants and friends as a one-man cheering squad. His energy knew no limits. Neither did his feats as a runner. To celebrate the year he turned 60 he ran 12 marathons and then ran an extra one for good measure. Thirteen marathons in 12 months. That was George!

In 1987 when I announced that I was running my first marathon George was there to tell me that I hadn't trained enough to do one so early in my running career. Instead of a "Doubting Thomas" I named him "Doubting George." We made a bet. If I finished the marathon he'd buy me a glass of wine. I did and he did!!!

The next year he again doubted my ability to complete the New York City Marathon. This time the ante was higher - a whole bottle of wine. I held up my end of the bargain but, not really being a drinker, opted for just another glass of wine and his heartfelt congratulations. Of course more of his running advice followed. Somehow I knew that he was secretly impressed by my running accomplishments. He never again made a bet with me.

In the last two years or so George's health diminished. Diagnosed with prostate cancer, his marathon running was reduced to three mile run-walks. Always fellow runners would be on hand to keep him company. For a short time he was able to resume some racing, albeit at a slower pace. Fellow runners enthusiastically cheered him on.

When conventional treatment didn't work George sought the unconventional, untried, and experimental methods. Running taught him to be a fighter. Rallying times became fewer, yet his eternal optimism never seemed to waiver. His litany of dos and don'ts for runners continued. So did the support of his family of runners in the community and beyond.

Despite a brave fight the voice of "The Guru" was soon stilled and his running feet stopped in their tracks. That is why I chose to remember him in my own special way. Yes, I ran one for George. It was a wonderfully serene eight miler.

I wrote this article because I felt all runners could identify with George. He was typical of what the running spirit was all about and of the bond and camaraderie that develops among runners.

The Mad Dash 1997

The Mad Dash 5K/10K races in Rhinebeck are a Labor Day tradition. This year I again looked forward to running the 10K race but it was not meant to be. As much as I gave it my best shot it turned out to be another DNF. I was sick and just wanted to go to sleep. I saw the race co-director before leaving, told him I was too ill to finish and had to drop out, and thanked him for a real nice event. It was then that he asked, "Could you write something about the Mad Dash?"

What can a runner say about dropping out of a race, not reaching the finish line, not meeting one's goal? What could I say about feeling plain lousy, defeated and sobbing when my husband met me? Soon these words by an unknown author came to mind: "Contentment is not the fulfillment of what you want, but the realization of how much you already have."

So I decided to write from my heart, why I ran it, why I am like other runners who pursue goals, and why I won't compromise my health or standards just to reach the finish line. One does not justify the other.

When I first ran the Mad Dash 10K in 1993 I thought it was the greatest thing going. It was so well organized, had an abundance of camaraderie, provided plenty of post-race refreshments, and gave lovely silver trophies to age group award winners. At the time I lived in a different county and knew Rhinebeck only as a spot on the map. The race director changed all that with giving me great written directions and her added notation "thanks for coming" on the postcard.

The year 1994 was a washout for me because of breathing problems which are now in the past. I ran the 10K well in 1995, albeit slower, but was happy to be a participant again. In 1996 I had thrown out my back (Lord knows how I did that!) a few days before the race and tried to run it anyway only to be forced to stop when severe pain overtook me. My fault. I chose not to heed my chiropractor's advice.

Let's face it. I like the Mad Dash. I like to run and I enjoy meeting so many different people from the running community. This was an event that I liked well enough to want to return to each year. It's my Labor Day tradition.

So why did I drop out? Let's just say I've been burning the candle at both ends and in between, pushing a going-on-60 body to the limit and beyond. If you've seen me in the past few months you can't help but notice that I have not bags under my eyes but steamer trunks! My commitments to my husband and family, to my widowed mother, and to my job are as steadfast as is my commitment to running. Therefore, I am super tired. A candidate for illness.

My mother's continued decline in health has brought about the need to actively participate in her home care needs. She lives over an hour driving time from my home and over two hours driving time from my place of employment. I spend more time on the roads in my car than I do running. Tires are wearing out faster than my running shoes. Yet I refuse to give up my running time and manage to squeeze it in somehow, sometime, somewhere, logging in 35-45 miles a week.

I'm not a candidate for sainthood. Rather I am a very tired runner trying to keep up with an unrealistic schedule. It has often meant getting four hours of sleep and rearranging hours on the job. My husband and I are like passing ships in the night, each anchoring at a different port. We try to train together on Sundays as a compromise for now.

While at my mother's country home I've discovered beautiful, peaceful running routes along the rural hilly backroads. I wave to scarecrows (if one ever waved back I'd make a mad dash of my own!), talk to woodchucks, dodge squirrels, admire an occasional deer, relish the fresh air and cherish this special country serenity. It's a time to forget life's demands. A time to run without any pressure. A time to reflect on how much I really do have.

A Runner's Special Thank You

"No act of kindness, no matter how small, is ever wasted." – Aesop, The Lion and the Mouse

It happened on a Saturday in June at a 10K race. The intense heat and humidity took its toll on me. I was also on the antibiotic tetracycline and ever so mindful of its effect of skin sensitization to the sun. At the four mile mark I felt like I was on fire, burning up and so very, very hot. When I felt that I was losing it I eased myself to the curb, lest a direct fall be injurious. It was heat exhaustion that wiped me out.

I recall a runner came over to me, losing precious race time to help a fallen fellow runner. Later on I learned that his name was Bill. There were also several others who stopped and expressed concern. To Bill, the medics, fellow runners and everyone who gave assistance, I am most grateful.

I run because I like to. I race because a little competitive voice encourages me to and I feel that I fit in with runners because of a special bond with the sport that unites us. However, I am overwhelmed at the selfless actions of runners like Bill. They are what makes the sport so meaningful to me. These actions warm my heart many times over.

We are so often shown the aggressiveness and meanness associated with some of the other sports. How nice it would be if people could be made aware of how runners take care of their own. We're not an elite bunch. We just have a sense of caring about others who share our love for running.

Cold, unfeeling hearts? I've seen just the opposite. For I am a runner.

Seasonal Disguises At Rockland Lake

Rockland Lake wears many "masks" as it changes with the seasons. Some are delightful and greeted with joy, others are greeted as challenges. All that one has to do to experience the myriad disguises is run - run with the wind, the rain, the sun, the snow - run all year 'round and remove each season's "masks."

SPRING bounces in with birds chirping, cool breezes, intermittent rainstorms, and dew drops on the grass. Everywhere a look of eager anticipation surveys the surroundings. Buds play peek-a-boo on the branches while the sun plays hide-and-seek with the clouds. Running in the pleasantly cool air has a soothing effect on the body. We pause to see the beginning of life everywhere. Running takes on its own special meaning.

SUMMER commences with an array of pastel colors - flowers are in full bloom, trees are no longer naked or partially dressed but rich with an abundance of leaves, and occasional rainbows add an artist's palette to the sky. The sun is warm and getting hotter. We feel the heat from the pavement and the sun's rays from the atmosphere. Perspiration drips profusely as we try to increase our pace. It's a time to run a little slower, drink a lot more water and enjoy a naturally-acquiring tan. As we run it is a time to envelop ourselves in all aspects of nature - its sounds, sights and smells.

FALL saunters in with a distinct crispness returning to the air. Trees take on a new field of colors - the browns, oranges, yellows and reds form a colorful wreath around the water's edge. Sunrises and sunsets add a finishing touch to Mother Nature's own majestical landscape. As we run, our strides tend to lengthen while we take in our magnificent surroundings. Fallen leaves cover the pavement and squish beneath our running shoes. A golden Midas Touch appears everywhere and a patchwork quilt of many colors emerges as fallen leaves amass on the ground. At times we run while the last remnant of the summer sun teases us with its quasi-warmth or the wind tosses us around like an aimlessly tossed football or a sudden cold rain shower greets us not too friendly. Still, we run on.

WINTER creeps in unexpectedly with its first snowfall. The lake becomes frozen and silent. Ice patches form and we soon learn the art of playing a game of "dodge 'em" as we run around the lake. Weeping willow trees wear glistening pearl necklaces as their icy branches hang downward. A surprise breeze makes them sound like musical wind chimes in the distance. We are running in our own winter wonderland. We feel a certain kind of rejuvenation from the cold, brisk air while we run to keep warm. Winter offers us challenges with its unpredictable weather and we delight in conquering our own running battles with these cruel elements of Mother Nature. We breathe out halos of cold air while we try to keep our hands and feet warm. The stillness of winter often lavishes an eerie effect as we hear our footstrikes crunching on the snow-covered paths. Leaving our footprints in the newly fallen snow, we become an invader in winter's territory. Winter running at the lake is definitely a rewarding challenge.

An Olympic Inspiration

Watching the recent Olympics and the Herculean efforts of the athletes can be awe-inspiring. For instance, take a couch potato and a runner viewing the men's marathon, an arduous trek from Marathon to Athens, Greece. The former will briefly think about getting up, then better reposition himself or herself to grab more munchies and beer. This shifting of positions may or may not involve much actual arm or leg movement. On the other hand I, the runner, may be inspired to get up and follow through on an unplanned run.

It was the fourth straight day of high temperatures (anything over 60 degrees is too hot for me) and a wickedly saturated atmosphere. Unbearable humidity, unbearable heat, and unbearable running conditions. Like being greeted by a geyser. After suffering for the previous three days with heavy legs that felt like stationary bedposts that were reluctant to move as I tried to run, scorching road pavements, and a sun so hot that it seemed to look down on me with an unfriendly hotter than hell appearance, I decided to forego any further punishment and not run. Facing utterly oppressive weather conditions once again had no appeal whatsoever this day. The runner in me was inert.

For me, the pause that refreshes was sitting in my rocker-recliner chair, soaking in the cool air-conditioned breezes and letting the marathoners take on the untamed heat and unforgiving hills. I marveled at their courage, their steady foot turnover, and their resolve to reach the finish at the stadium in Athens.

The hills were torturous, yet splits of a tad over five minutes per mile emerged. Pheidippides would have been proud! I was inspired.

I remained glued to the TV, comfortably cool and still comfortably inert. American runner Meb Keflezighi was gaining ground on the lead pack, his leg movements so synchronized and fluid. My legs were synchronized in the stretched out position to accommodate a snoozing feline. Fluid leg movement was not to be. God forbid I should awaken a sleeping cat!! I continued watching the runners. My own adrenaline was soon approaching high gear as I watched the finish, with the American earning a well-deserved silver medal. My inertness was being replaced by so much excitement. How fast things change. The cat must go.

It must have been that imagined high level of adrenaline or a moment of sheer stupidity that overtook me on this "dog day of summer." Since neither heat nor humidity bother Roy, he decided to do an ambitious seven mile run, regardless of the choking moisture in the air and the sun's strong rays. In a moment of non-lucidity I decided why not me, too? My humble expectation was to do a short but hilly 3.4 mile route. No heroics for me at 2:30 in the afternoon. We left a few minutes apart, going in opposite directions. Shortly thereafter, I was surprised to see Roy running my planned route in reverse. He chose to bow to the unrelenting Gods of Heat.

In the end, we were soaked to the core and Rancid Man Roy lived up to his name. You could pour the salty liquid from his running shoes! We reached the same conclusion that our run was slowness in motion and oppressively unbearable. But hey, we did it! Call it an Olympic inspiration run.

Attitude Adjustment

My attitude was if I can't run it, I'll work it. Thus, it was a real attitude adjustment for me when I volunteered, along with Roy, to be part of the traffic control team for the Dutchess County Classic Marathon. We had earlier decided to respectively do the full and half marathon at Schroon Lake a mere week later. Missing out as a Classic marathon participant would be a heartbreaker for me. However, I knew that my aged legs couldn't take the beating of back-to-back 26.2 milers.

It was not until race day that it really hit me. I was not running!! When we arrived at our assigned posts, my thoughts drifted back to all the times that I ran along this segment of the course. I tried not to let tears of nostalgia overtake me. My attitude adjustment wasn't working too well. I yearned to be at the starting line-up.

As soon as the runners started coming, it was time to get my attitude adjustment and do my assigned task. The thrill of being there intensified as more and more runners came by. I cheered for them all, many of whom I knew. A few quizzically uttered, "You're not running?" A few times I said, "I'd rather be running." As for their many words of gratitude and smiles? Priceless. I told the marathoners that I'd see them again on their second loop. Mentally I was also running the marathon route.

What a thrill it was to see the first marathoner pass by on his second loop! He was a solitary figure with unforgettable speed and leg stride. It was 10:42 AM.

Nostalgia again set in when a runner wearing bib #1 passed, as this had long been my assigned bib number for the marathon. Another early runner seemed to be struggling a bit, so I was taken by surprise when he asked me, "How are you doing?" The leading woman at the time had bib #21, which is my lucky number. It is also symbolic because my three adult sons have a notion that their mother is "eternally 21." I smiled because my attitude was so positive now. However, I still imagined at certain times where I would be on the course. A runner wearing bib #18 passed by and cheerfully said, "I remember you."

Traffic had picked up and was really bad at times. Many vehicles didn't slow down or drove over the white line onto the shoulder. I guarded my spot with subdued defiance. Although my red baseball cap said "New York Blood Center," I had no intention of being someone's roadkill. I continued to caution the runners.

Around 11 AM the traffic control coordinator drove up - with FOOD!!! It was good to see him smiling and more relaxed than earlier in the morning. I selected a fruit drink, apple, banana, and plain bagel. Shortly thereafter a runner, now walking and obviously in discomfort, passed by. I offered him my lunch and he gratefully took the fruit drink and banana. I could only hope that he had enough stamina to reach the finish line with about 11 more miles to go.

Shortly before noontime, a smiling woman runner said to me, "You're 20. I keep telling myself I have only 6 more to go." Taken aback by her words, I looked down to see if I had the number 20 somewhere on my bright orange vest. A guy running behind her sheepishly grinned and he said to me, "It's only 15 here." I chuckled. He was right.

By about 12:40 PM the field of runners dwindled to one lone walker who was determined to reach the finish line. I wished her well and recalled the many times that I had to reach deep down into my inner core of strength and determination to make it to the finish. I also knew that my attitude adjustment was successful. You see, there's always next year.

My Lucky Race Items

Being a retired Research and Development Scientist/Chemist, two things may seem contradictory to scientific dictums: (1) that I rely on woolly caterpillars (not the Old Farmer's Almanac) for winter weather predictions and (2) that I do wear my "lucky race items."

In my wristband I carry a round silver medallion given to me by a special running friend. It has the cutout image of an angel with the words "Guardian Angel" on one side and "Sent to Watch Over You" on the other side.

Attached to the laces on my racing shoes I have a metal Road Runner ID tag, which has my medical information. Although this was more necessary during my solitary long races, it's been such a long time "lucky" racing item that its importance is still relevant.

Lastly, when I returned to running with a bad knee in early 2011, I found luck and inspiration in wearing a pink fleece cap with the letters MT in blue and Middle Tennessee in smaller white letters on the front. It was a gift from my youngest son and his wife. Because wearing it got me through those early rough days, it will continue to be a part of my "lucky" colder weather racing attire. Of course, should I wear it in hot weather races, don't think that I've lost my scientific marbles . . . yet!

No Recognition at 70 Plus

I am writing about an issue that is of concern to us 70 plus seniors, particularly woman runners, who are up there in years but still young at heart. That we are not usually recognized for awards in our own age group is an insult to all of us.

Through the years we've become slower runners, no longer the speedy front locomotive but the last slow caboose. Yet, we are still active racers. We put our aching and aging bones and bodies (and all other parts in between!) to the test every time we set foot on the pavement. We persevere, overlooking nagging injuries, tired bodies, sore bones and over-used feet and reach the finish line, not with a bang but with a determined heart. The clock's fast ticking has added time (in years) to our age while giving us slower (in minutes) finish times. To use Roy's words of self-description, "I may not be fast but I am slow." This describes us 70 + women runners who still feel that we've earned our "days in the sun" at races at whatever pace we move.

The lack of proper age group recognition upsets us because competing against 60 year olds is unfair. I was still quite fast at 60 but got really slow at 70. I am far removed from the 60 year old age group. Why are there 70 plus categories for men while we, as women, are relegated to the "60 and over" group? There isn't even any age group recognition for 80 plus athletes, male or female. This, too, should not continue. Just look at how robust and healthy some senior runners are.

In a society where youth and fast racing times take center stage, what becomes of those of us who were once youthful and fast or younger and faster than we are now? Young, fast age group winners are the first called up for their recognition. It's a long wait for the 70 plus woman runners. We heartily applaud the efforts of those before us while we wait and wait for our turn. Few are left to applaud for us as most participants have left by time we might get some accolades. The oldest women are always the last called. Often, as I have experienced, there are not even any awards left for us. Certainly never a morale booster. As a courtesy, wouldn't it be appropriate to recognize older (male and female) runners first? Good manners at least!

This age group disparity for women has been brought to my attention on numerous occasions.

Let's stop the emphasis on youth and speed and recognize equally all ages and all times. Sometimes there may be only one runner in our age group, so why should we be shut out? We still are bona fide competitors. Proper recognition may inspire more "older folks" to enter races. There is no shame in walking or running at a turtle's pace. Roy still chuckles with fond memories at his "Turtle Award," a unique glass obelisk with a turtle figure nearing the top, given to him at the 2005 Bocchino Brothers Firefighter 10K Race. He was last but certainly not least. It is no shame to be old or slow. We are not afraid to hide our age or to get less joy out of our accomplishments.

High Spirits

It was a 5K race with a 3K walk to honor and remember a beloved teacher, friend to all, and a dedicated race scorer, as well as to support funds for programs for youth. However, the Gods of Good Weather did not make an appearance that day in May. Thus, with a steady rainfall and high humidity, it meant that we all had to "go with the flow." To paraphrase a saying, it rained on everyone's parade that day. However, one's spirits were not diminished.

Despite the unkind whims of Mother Nature, many volunteers, course marshals, timing crew, and emergency medical personnel had to tackle the business at hand so that eager participants of all ages could reach the finish line. The well-marked course was blissfully devoid of any traffic and gas fumes, traversing an area on the scenic and serene grounds at a religious facility. However, the race route was unsuspectingly an eye opener, a quads-acher, and a fortitude tester. Participants had to conquer a very hilly one mile loop three times before being able to say, "I did it!" at the finish line. I did silently utter, "Oh, Lord!" many times with each uphill trek. When done, although at a much slower pace than usual, I grinned from ear to ear with my turtle time of 40:47. Hey, I did come in before midnight and even won a beautiful silver age group medal. When I related that my 79th birthday was coming up shortly, the announcer from a popular radio station asked everyone present to join him in serenading me with the "Happy Birthday" song, followed by an enthusiastic round of applause! How can anything top this?

It was fun and challenging to test my limits and be grateful that I only had to run 3.1 miles in these wet conditions. Although I have earned my wrinkles, I did not want the steady rainfall to transform me into a soggy, wrinkled-looking prune. A wrinkled prune look will possibly have to come at a later date and at a longer distance during another downpour. I am in no hurry to make this happen.

Doing My Best

George Sheehan once wrote: "It does not matter where I finish or how fast I run. Being a winner means doing my best."

This is how it is with me now. My bad knees control how I run. No more sonic boom finishes. No more up front pace with the leaders. No more long fluid strides or running with the ease of a wild stallion (in my case a mare). I can't relive the past or dwell on what once was. I can only run as the present allows me to do, sometimes being the caboose in a race and no longer traveling in the fast lane that I loved for so many years.

If doing my best means that I'm a winner, a slower pace won't deter me. Sometimes I may feel like a failure when heat and humidity or hills get the best of me and my racing goals are compromised, meaning I am slower than slow. Then I remind myself, if I do my best, I can reach the finish line, however slow I may be.

My best now means being cognizant of where and how I plant my feet, avoiding uneven sidewalks and curbs whenever possible, treading cautiously on rocky or pebbly paths, walking when I need to, and doing it all in slower movements. This is viewed positively because it gives me a chance to be on the course for a longer time to enjoy my surroundings. Doing my best, albeit slow, means laughing more, listening to chirping birds, watching the ugly, clumsy klutzenflappers and their ungraceful movements, pausing to admire a pretty fragrant wildflower, or getting soaked in a downpour. It means staying within my limitations while running and being appreciative of what I can still do rather than bemoan what I can no longer do. If I am doing my best, I'll always be a winner. That works for me.

Epilogue

It is with an abundance of wonderment and sheer gratitude that I look back on more than thirty years of running that have molded the senior athlete that I am today. The carefree and gay abandon attitude of my earlier years of running and bicycling have been replaced by a much more cautionary approach to all athletic activities. My older body and bones have lost their flexibility but the desire for an adventurous life is still present.

The route that I took towards becoming a runner had many twists and turns, uncountable ups and downs, and numerous uncertainties. Not to take a risk is not to be open to the joys of success or the availability of lessons to be learned from failure. Each experience enhances one's growth and self-confidence in different ways. How we choose to learn determines our next step as a growing person. Becoming a runner did all this for me and gave me an outlet to emerge as a confident, happy and successful person. Those earlier words "Go for it, Mom" made all the difference in my long journey to becoming a runner.

However, just when I thought it couldn't get any better, it happened, and life reached another special pinnacle. Roy and I were joined by the three "boys," David, Paul, and Greg, and for the first time ever, we were all together at the same place, at the same time and running in the same race. The date was February 19, 2017, the venue was Danbury, Connecticut, and the race was The Big Chili 5K. Many factors came together to make it happen with distances being bridged and all aches and pains being left by the wayside. It was a once-in-a-lifetime family memory where we all reached the finish line standing up and smiling.

Addendum - Records

Eleanor Roosevelt once said, "You must do the thing you think you cannot do." With this in mind and with feelings of trepidation and anxiety, I chose to stand tall at the starting line of all races. These personal race records at various ages helped put me at the pinnacle of my incredible running journey.

Distance	Clock Time	Age
1 Mile	7:04	59
	7:07	62
	8:08	69
	8:21	70
	9:42	73
	10:14	78
2 Miles	13:53	59
5K (3.1 Miles)	21:36	54
	21:55	54
	25:39	64
	28:50	70
	33:52	78
5 Miles	35:17	55
	36:08	55
	45:47	67
	46:56	69
	57:50	79
10K (6.2 Miles)	43:42	54
	43:53	55
	53:15	63
	54:39	65
	1:01:14	70

Distance	Clock Time	Age
15K (9.3 Miles)	1:09:58	52
	1:10:57	54
	1:23:16	65
	1:38:37	70
10 Miles	1:16:23	56
	1:17:28	52
	1:22:03	58
	1:32:11	65
	1:43:22	69
	1:48:58	70
Half Marathon (13.1 Miles)	1:39:32	53
	1:39:37	55
	2:15:00	68
	2:29:03	71
25K (15.5 Miles)	2:00:54	54
	2:01:46	55
	2:33:47	65
30K (18.6 Miles)	2:28:47	55
	3:07:48	64
	3:50:13	69

Marathons and Ultras – see "Catching the Running Spirit" in Chapter 13 for "pinnacles."

Other Times:

Marathon (26.2 Miles)	3:52:11	57
	4:03:10	58
	4:03:54	52
	4:23:19	63
	4:42:56	66
50K (31.1 Miles)	5:11:49	51
	5:16:36	52
	6:04:53	65
	6:36:17	69

www.ingramcontent.com/pod-product-compliance
Lightning Source LLC
Chambersburg PA
CBHW020417010526
44118CB00010B/289